The Ukulele Handbook

The Ukulele Handbook

Gavin Pretor-Pinney & Tom Hodgkinson

BLOOMSBURY

LONDON · NEW DELHI · NEW YORK · SYDNEY

For Verity

First published in Great Britain 2013
Copyright © 2013 by Gavin Pretor-Pinney and Tom Hodgkinson
For picture credits, see page 140.

Bloomsbury Publishing Plc
50 Bedford Square
London WC1B 3DP

www.bloomsbury.com

Bloomsbury Publishing, London, New Delhi, New York and Sydney

A CIP catalogue record for this book is available
from the British Library.
Library of Congress Cataloging-in-Publication Data has been applied for.

ISBN 978 1 4088 3629 3
US ISBN 978 1 62040 220 7

10 9 8 7 6 5 4 3 2 1

Design by Gavin Pretor-Pinney

All papers used by Bloomsbury are natural, recyclable products made from wood grown in
well-managed forests. The manufacturing processes conform to the environmental regulations
of the country of origin.

Printed and bound by South China Printing Company, Dongguan, Guangdong

(Frontispiece) *Kolomona: Hawaiian Troubadour* (1808) by Hubert Vos. Kolomona was
a worker in the Honolulu docks by day and a popular ukulele entertainer by night.

Contents

A Four-string Revolution

THIS IS THE story of a small guitar that charmed the world. The ukulele – just a little wooden box with four strings stretched over it – is the most unassuming of instruments, but it has led a rich and turbulent life. It has been praised by kings and ridiculed by wags. It has been embraced by millions one year, only to be rejected and forgotten the next. But through its changing fortunes the uke has shown great resilience and longevity: just when you think it has died forever, it pops back up again, full of vigour, ready to win new friends.

The ukulele's charm lies in its democratic nature. Anyone can play it, so we can all become music-makers. Its cheerful sound makes people smile. It is also astonishingly versatile: from the Sex Pistols to Bach, it lends itself to every type of music.

As a teaching tool, the uke is unsurpassed. Time and again it has been used to introduce children to the rudiments of music-making. And even the most unmusical of adults find they can start making a reasonable sound within just a few minutes of picking it up.

Nothing lends itself better to convivial activity, to music performed for its own sake, just for the sheer joy of playing and singing in a group. The uke offers a creative outlet that can free you from your worries. For many people it has provided a livelihood too: they manufacture ukuleles, produce songbooks or give live performances.

Ancestors of this modest but strangely powerful instrument can be traced back to the Renaissance, when the first small guitars were made in Europe. Ukulele-like instruments also appear in 18th-century prints. In the late 19th century a descendant of these early small guitars, the four-string *machete*, migrated halfway round the world, from the Portuguese island of Madeira to Hawaii, where the people were captivated by its charm. There it evolved into the ukulele and peacefully colonized the planet.

The cast of characters involved in its fascinating story includes Edward Lear, Lewis Carroll, Robert Louis Stevenson, the last King and Queen of Hawaii, Nancy Mitford, Marilyn Monroe, Elvis Presley, George Harrison, Kermit the Frog and Warren Buffett, as well as the more familiar uke gods, such as George Formby and Israel Kamakawiwo'ole.

We both took up the uke around 2007, and found it such a pleasure that we became evangelical about it, and even started up a ukulele orchestra. That same enthusiasm has produced this book, which aims to be both an illustrated history and a primer, and which we hope will be enjoyed by uke fans and create a few more.

The story of the uke is one of technological progress. Its First Wave of popularity, in the Twenties, was fuelled by radio. The Second Wave, in the Fifties, was enabled by television and by new developments in plastics technology. And the Third Wave – the one we are riding today – was given a massive boost by the Internet, which makes it so easy to share songs, tips and performances with the world.

The ukulele embodies the Hawaiian concept of *aloha*, which can be translated as 'good cheer' and 'openness'. Even in its very early days, the instrument spoke of a release from work and worry: it promised love, frivolity, living in the moment and better times. All these things are embodied in the iconography of the ukulele – little boats, moonlight, beaches and rocks beside the sea. It's escapism at its most charming. Little wonder, then, that the uke has always had romantic associations: ukulele sheet music covers of the Twenties tended to picture a scantily clad girl in a grass skirt dancing in the light of the moon or underneath a palm tree, by the sea or in a boat, while the boy lightly strums his uke. In fact, the girl is often seen crooning to the boy, making the uke a feminist instrument even way back then.

There is also a political dimension to the history of the ukulele. Whether in the hands of King Kalakaua in the late 19th century, or 'King' Israel Kamakawiwo'ole in the late 20th, the uke has played a role in Hawaii as an upholder of the old ways against the forces of missionaries and modernization, while also being manipulated by commercial interests for its obvious potential as a tourist gimmick. The jovial George Formby showed a serious side when he protested against apartheid by playing to black audiences in South Africa. And today musician Paul Moore is attempting to use the power of the uke to bring peace to Palestine.

As history shows, the happy sound of the ukulele brings people together. All over the world people are joining workshops, clubs, bands and societies to play the uke and sing. Lifelong friendships have been formed at these sessions, which put the power of music creation into the hands of the people. Those who previously considered themselves unmusical have been amazed at how quickly their playing abilities develop, and how much fun they have while doing so. Remember, these groups get together just for pleasure and the joy of playing.

Once you've learned a few chords and strums in our six-week ukulele course (see page 77), you can turn to our songbook (see page 117), which features classic tunes, ranging from 'Greensleeves' to 'Scarborough Fair' and 'Waltzing Matilda'. Get these fourteen songs under your belt and you will have the beginnings of a rich musical treasury.

So join the uke revolution, and spread joy and good cheer wherever you go.

Gavin Pretor-Pinney and Tom Hodgkinson
July 2013

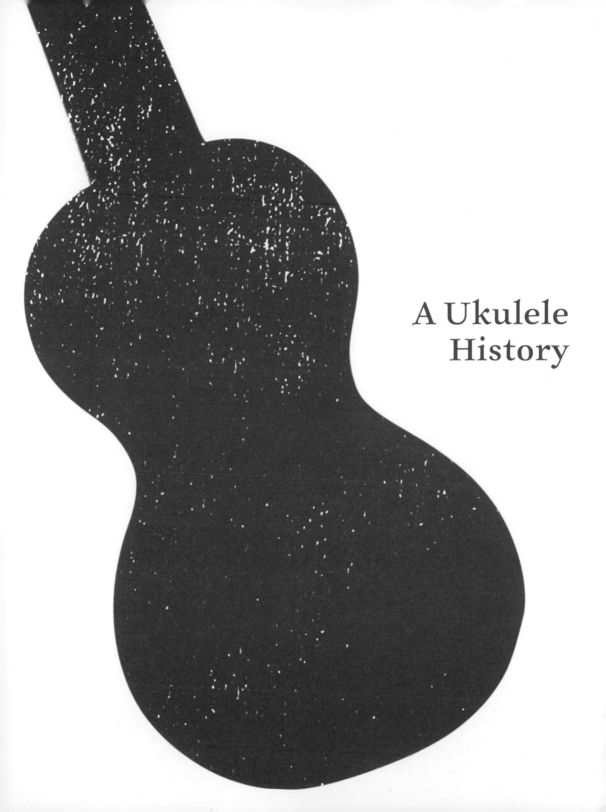

A Ukulele History

Ancestors of the Uke

WHILE THE UKULELE was officially born in Hawaii in 1879, the history of small guitars goes back a lot further, to 15th-century Europe, when a guitar craze erupted during the Renaissance. Thanks to the printing press, teach-yourself manuals were widely distributed, and guitars of all shapes and sizes were created. The *chitarrino*, for example, was an Italian instrument that had four pairs or 'courses' of strings and was often tuned in exactly the same way as the modern ukulele, with a higher top string, a tuning known as 're-entrant'. About 300 years later, in the baroque period, we find the ukulele-like *mandola*, a small mandolin with four strings.

The small guitar appears in the Victorian era too. An 1858 photo by Charles L. Dodgson, better known as the nonsense writer Lewis Carroll, shows Alice Liddell, inspiration for the Wonderland stories, and her two sisters holding tiny guitars. These are in fact *machetes*, the very same instrument from the Portuguese island of Madeira that later evolved into the uke. The girls are wearing Madeiran lace, so we guess that someone in the family had been on holiday to Madeira and brought back the *machetes* and dresses as souvenirs.

The small guitar also appealed to Edward Lear, that other great Victorian writer of nonsense verse. We all know the lines from his 1867 poem 'The Owl and the Pussycat':

The owl looked up to the stars above
And sang to a small guitar

Could the 'small guitar' that Edward Lear drew (top) to accompany his poem 'The Owl and the Pussycat' have been a precursor to the ukulele?

Lewis Carroll's 1858 photograph (above) shows Alice Liddell, of Wonderland fame, with her sisters Lorina and Edith, holding *machetes* from Madeira (below).

Lear was very well travelled and is likely to have seen a small guitar on his excursions. In his illustration the poem's lovers are making their escape from the hurly-burly, and the charming fowl is holding a small guitar-like instrument high up as he croons.

Both images opposite demonstrate something of the unassuming and eccentric charm of the ukulele. Already you can see the attractions of the instrument: it looks cute, it is suitable for children, and it is a handy size to carry in a small boat. In this context it also has connotations of escape, of an island paradise – the sort of fantasy destination that the alienated Owl and Pussycat might well have dreamt of running away to. And Madeira was a popular holiday destination for stressed-out Brits, just as Hawaii would later become to stressed-out Americans.

The music of pre-ukulele Hawaii was influenced by missionaries and other visitors, who introduced hymn singing and various instruments, including the bass viol, violin and guitar. Old customs, such as chanting and *hula* dancing, were discouraged by the Christians as they carried pagan associations.

This 1716 illustration shows a young dude plucking a ukulele-like *mandola* on the beach. The iconography is strikingly similar to ukulele images that would proliferate 200 years later.

Jolly Madeiran country musicians (top) depicted in William Coombe's *A History of Madeira* (1821) include one on the left playing a *machete*. Might the musician on the right, playing a six-stringed *viola francesa*, have spent a little too long getting ready in front of the mirror?

The missionary preaching (above) to a group of Hawaiians in the kukui groves (1841) was presumably not declaiming the virtues of traditional Hawaiian *hula* ceremonies.

In 1819, as a result of European influence, the old Hawaiian religion of *kapu* was abolished. In 1826 the *Missionary Herald* reported: 'There are still ... multitudes who continue in rather a secret manner to worship their old false gods, but their number is every month growing less.'

Another popular musical import was the waltz, introduced by ship bands. In 1872 the Royal Hawaiian Band, led by a Prussian named Henry Berger, introduced the island to European music by the likes of Richard Strauss and Giuseppe Verdi. He was patronized by the island's king, David Kalakaua, a great music fan known as the 'Merry Monarch'. Always open to new styles, influences and ideas, the king would later play a key role in the story of the ukulele.

If the missionaries and modernizers had had their way, old Hawaiian culture and music would have been wiped out completely. Oddly enough, it was a foreign instrument – the *machete* – that was to play a key role in reviving some of the old Hawaiian customs.

The Uke is Born

THE ukulele was born in Hawaii on 23 August 1879. It was on that day that the *Ravenscrag*, a ship bearing 419 immigrants from the Portuguese island of Madeira, docked in Honolulu harbour. In the 1840s Madeira had fallen prey to poverty and famine as a result of crop failures and political instability, so its inhabitants were leaving in droves in search of better fortune elsewhere. At the same time, an underpopulated Hawaii was looking for workers to exploit the potential of its sugar plantations. The authorities appointed a German named William Hillebrand to look for a source of new labour, and in 1877 he chose Madeira, reporting: 'In my opinion your islands could not possibly get a more desirable class of Immigrants than the population of the Madeira and Azore Islands. Sober, honest, industrious and peaceable, they combine all the qualities of a good settler, and with all this, they are inured to your climate.' Hillebrand subsequently produced a pamphlet selling Hawaii's virtues to the Madeirans, and it worked. Boatloads of Portuguese started to arrive in Honolulu harbour.

What no one could have predicted, however, was that the Madeirans would make a contribution to Hawaiian musical culture that would travel the world over the next century and beyond. For as they boarded the boat, they took with them their little four-string

Machetes like those shown above, made in Madeira during the 1850s, were taken to Hawaii aboard the *Ravenscrag*, which docked in Honolulu harbour (below) in 1879.

Tourist postcards of the 1880s, showing Hawaiian maidens with ukes and guitars. The grass skirts, bare breasts, *leis* (flower garlands), mud huts, palm trees and distant mountaintops are all there, but someone's forgotten to tell them to smile.

guitars, or *machetes*, the instrument that would turn into the ukulele.

It is generally agreed that *Ravenscrag* passenger João Fernandes was the first to play the *machete* in Hawaii. He himself wrote that he 'strummed away to his heart's content' to celebrate the ship's safe arrival. The Madeirans lost no time in pursuing their traditional custom of wandering around singing and playing their small guitars, and the Hawaiians, ever open to new ideas, were delighted. Just two weeks after the arrival of the *Ravenscrag* the local newspaper reported:

> *During the past week a band of Portuguese musicians, composed of Madeira Islanders recently arrived here, have been delighting the people with nightly street concerts. The musicians are true performers on their strange instruments, which are a kind of cross between a guitar and a banjo, but which produce very sweet music in the hands of the Portuguese minstrels. We confess to having enjoyed the music ourselves and hope to hear more of it.*

That they did. Hawaii was instantly swept up in a *machete* craze. Three of the Madeirans – Manuel Nunes, Augusto Dias and José do Espirito Santo – were skilled furniture-makers, and within a few years of their arrival, they had set up shop as ukulele-makers. The tuning of the *machete* was adjusted to g, C, E, A, the first string being a high note.

Before the name 'ukulele' caught hold, the *machete* was referred to by Hawaiians as a 'taropatch fiddle'. Taro is a tuberous root vegetable widely grown on the island, so it is likely that the handily portable instrument was taken to the fields by those working the land and played during their rest periods.

But not everyone got the point of these small guitars, as reported in 1886:

The early ukuleles above show the distinctive styles of their makers – the one on the left by Manuel Nunes, and the one on the right by José do Espirito Santo. The adverts (left) from the Honolulu *Evening Bulletin* make them sound boringly identical.

Manuel Nunes (1843–1922)

'INVENTOR OF THE ORIGINAL UKULELE'

It is the moustachioed Madeiran immigrant Manuel Nunes who is credited with transforming the *machete* into the ukulele. This he did by changing the body shape, and altering the tuning to the 're-entrant' g, C, E, A. He arrived in Honolulu in 1879, when aged 36, with his eighteen-year-old wife and four children from his previous marriage. There the couple produced five more offspring.

After fulfilling his contract to work the sugar plantations, Nunes started making ukuleles in 1880, and continued for the next 40 years. In the local business directory he described himself as 'inventor of the original ukulele', and his sons followed him into the business. One of his apprentices went on to found his own ukulele company, which bears his name to this day. Nunes died aged 79 and is buried in Honolulu's King Street cemetery.

M. NUNES
Inventor of the
original

Ukulele

Patronized by the

Royal Hawaiian Family

Manufactured by

M. Nunes & Sons
76 S. Beretania St.
P. O. Box 1145
Honolulu, T. H.

Manuel Nunes, prolific creator of ukuleles and babies, traded on his royal patronage – in the case of this 1916 newspaper advertisement, nearly a quarter century after the abolition of the Hawaiian monarchy.

[Hawaiians] are exceptionally fond of the guitar, and they play it as a solo instrument, with a tenderness, a softness which speaks well for the delicacy of their feelings ... of late they have taken to the banjo and to that hideous small Portuguese instrument now called [the] 'taropatch fiddle'.

Despite such snobbish comments, the ukulele's popularity spread with amazing speed, and in 1888, just ten years after its arrival, it was being described as 'the national instrument of Hawaii'.

The origins of the word 'ukulele' (pronounced 'oo-koo-lay-lee' in the Hawaiian language) are still a little misty. While *uku* literally means 'insect' and *lele* means 'to fly', author Jack London wrote in *The Cruise of the Snark* (1911) that '*ukulele* is the Hawaiian for "jumping flea", as it is also the Hawaiian for a certain musical instrument that may be likened to a young guitar'. This remains the most popular theory, though Queen Lili'uokalani's preferred explanation is that the word is derived from the Hawaiian meaning 'a gift from over there'.

(Above) Hawaiian musicians uked up and ready to *hula*, *c.*1900.

(Below) 'All back to mine?' Iolani Palace, pictured in 1880, was where King David Kalakaua, the 'Merry Monarch', held his weekly poker nights, with music performed on the fashionable new ukulele.

King David Kalakaua (1836–91)

ROYAL PATRON AND COMPOSER

King David Kalakaua is one of the most important figures in Hawaiian music, presiding as he did over the island's cultural renaissance at the end of the 19th century. He was brought up to learn old Hawaiian chants, and popularized them during his reign, which led to contemporary missionaries accusing him of falling back into paganism.

Undaunted by such comments, he included the *hula* dance in ceremonies to mark both his belated coronation in 1883 and his jubilee in 1886. He believed that the survival of his kingdom depended on his people connecting with their own ancient culture. However, as well as upholding ancient Hawaiian traditions, he was also a fan of novelty, and enthusiastically promoted the ukulele in the years following its arrival on the island. In particular, he patronized ukulele-maker Augusto Dias, whom he permitted to stamp a royal crown on every instrument he made. King David's own compositions include 'Hawai'i Pono'i' (1874) and 'Koni au I Ka Wai', and thanks to his leadership, the 1880s and 1890s were musically lively decades.

Given to luxury and grandeur, he spent $300,000 on building Iolani Palace. However, in 1887 he was forced at gunpoint to sign a new constitution by the Hawaiian League, who were in favour of annexation by the United States. The king died in San Francisco in 1891, and on his deathbed is reported to have said: 'Tell my people I tried.'

King David (below, far left) chilling beside his friend Robert Louis Stevenson in 1889. The author of *Treasure Island* was a regular guest at Iolani Palace. Here they are being entertained by the King's Singing Boys with ukulele accompaniment.

LIKELY TO HAPPEN UNDER THE COMING ADMINISTRATION.

THE ANNEXATION HUSTLERS IN HAWAII WILL START A GENUINE AMERICAN REAL ESTATE BOOM, AND REAP ALL THE PROFITS THERE ARE IN IT.

The satirical cartoon above, from *Puck* magazine in 1897, depicts the Americans taking over Hawaii. It shows Sanford B. Dole, 'President of the Republic of Hawaii', conducting a land auction of property he probably does not own.

King Kalakaua booked uke-players for his weekly poker parties at the opulent Iolani Palace, which became a hub for traditional Hawaiian culture. João Fernandes apparently said that he and his mates were often invited to the palace for parties at which there were 'plenty *kanakas* [Hawaiians]. Much music, much *hula*, much *kaukau* [food], much drink. All time plenty drink. And King Kalakaua, he pay for all'.

A regular guest at these *soirées* was none other than Robert Louis Stevenson, who played the flute and was a lover of the laid-back Hawaiian ways. In 1889, according to his wife Fanny, he took a *machete* with him on a trip to Samoa. She describes 'a native instrument something like a banjo, called a taropatch fiddle'.

The king, who had learned about ancient Hawaiian music from his grandmother, and about modern music while at school, soon learned to play the uke and began to compose songs. Robert Louis Stevenson's step-daughter wrote: '[The king] would occasionally pick up a ukulele or guitar and sing his favourite Hawaiian song, "Sweet Lei-lei-hua".' David's sister Lydia, who would later become Queen Lili'uokalani, also learned the instrument and wrote songs for it, some of which are played to this day.

It is not until 1890 that scholars can find a printed reference to the uke, and this first mention of the word uses a different spelling. Tourist Helen Mathew described a tea party in Honolulu, the capital of Hawaii, where 'native musicians, on the guitar, violin, taropatch, and ukelele [sic], were rendering delightful music'.

In 1893 Hawaii was taken over by a group of European and American businessmen, who deposed the monarchy with the help of US marines, and created a republic. This was a sort of bloodless coup called the 'Annexation'. The following year President Grover Cleveland admitted that the overthrow was illegal, but the monarchy never returned. In 1993, the Clinton administration apologized for the overthrow, but the damage was done and could not be rectified. To this day, Hawaiians look back to the last days of the monarchy as a time of self-government and self-determination. In today's Hawaii, to praise the king and queen and the old ways is a gesture of radical defiance against commercial exploitation of the islands by North American interests.

It was around the end of the 19th century that Hawaii began to market itself as a tourist destination, and the ukulele was to become a key feature in its PR efforts. The instrument came to epitomize Hawaii's love of leisure and a good time, clearly an attractive fantasy to the workers in a rapidly industrializing United States. It is to this era that we can date the first appearance of that iconic Hawaiian image – a fresh-faced girl wearing a *lei* and a grass skirt, her hair adorned with flowers, while sitting on a beach, idly strumming her uke. Modernization had attacked the old ways, but now a commercial imperative brought them back.

The ukulele became an export product. In 1893 Hawaii took a delegation to the World's Columbia Exposition in Chicago, where a reporter observed that the ukulele instantly became fashionable with the younger crowd searching for authenticity amid their urban alienation. As he colourfully noted:

Hula

The *hula* is the traditional dance form of Hawaii. Originally a religious rite, it eventually became a way of teaching and a form of entertainment. It is also used as the foundation for the *lua*, the Hawaiian art of self-defence. The *hula* is supposed to honour the gods, remind Hawaiians about their great nobility, and to teach perfection in dancing. Famously witnessed by Captain Cook in 1778, it takes its inspiration from nature. According to the authoritative work *Hawaiian Music and Musicians* (2012): 'The hula was performed on occasions to invoke the gods at births, feasts, weddings, and funerals. Wars, spells, charms, incantation, and just sheer entertainment gave reason for the performance of the hula.' A visitor in 1798 said of a group of 200 *hula* dancers: 'The whole of this numerous group was in perfect unison of voice and action ... They exhibited great ease and much elegance, and the whole was executed with a degree of correctness not easily to be imagined.' What groovy natives! The *hula* declined throughout the 19th century as the missionaries considered it superstitious.

A member of the Royal Hawaiian Girls Glee Club, c.1935.

Queen Lili'uokalani (1838–1917)

MONARCH AND COMPOSER

Lili'uokalani, King David Kalakaua's sister, started her musical training at the age of four and became probably the most gifted Hawaiian musician of her time. She composed hundreds of songs, and wrote: 'I scarcely remember the days when it would not have been possible for me to write either the words or the music for any occasion on which poetry or song was needed. To compose was as natural to me as to breathe.' Her favourite instrument was the zither, but she also played the ukulele, guitar and organ. Her great gift was to combine Hawaiian and Western musical forms, which in the 1890s led Mathias Gray & Co. of San Francisco to publish 25 of her songs. She had a Stateside hit with 'Aloha Oe', which means 'Farewell to thee'. Ostensibly a love song – it inspired a Jack London story of the same name about a doomed love affair, and Elvis Presley sang a version of it in the film *Blue Hawaii* (1961) – some commentators believe she was saying goodbye to sovereignty; she acceded to the throne in 1891 but was deposed by republicans just two years later. While on a trip to Washington DC in the late 1890s, the queen described how an American girl 'sang some of my own Hawaiian songs to [the accompaniment of] our instrument, the ukulele, [and] gave me that joy, so sadly sweet, of listening to the sounds of home in foreign lands'.

(Above) A sheet music cover for 'Aloha Oe', the great hit that Queen Lili'uokalani wrote in 1877 or 1878.

(Below) Once you become queen, you get a better chair.

Aloha

Few would dispute that *aloha* is the most internationally recognized Hawaiian word, but equally few would be able to offer a definition. It generally connotes the typically Hawaiian characteristics of love, affection, openness and generosity, but in song it has been taken to mean 'hello', 'farewell', 'sweetheart', 'kindness' and 'charity'. Some claim that *aloha* is merely a promotional gimmick cooked up by Hawaii's tourist industry, but the sociologist Andrew Lind has argued that it describes 'a temperamental disposition' of the islanders. In fact, visitors to Hawaii always remark on the island hospitality or '*aloha* spirit' they find there.

The stroller along the Midway Plaisance ... is greeted by no more alluring sound than the sweet strains from the 'taro patch fiddle', banjo, and guitar skillfully played by native musicians ... the soft melody of native airs and songs has awakened more than a transient response in the breasts of our sentimental music lovers and no small number of fair pupils from San Francisco's 'swell set' have been for weeks industriously practicing the 'taro patch fiddle' under the tuition of the dusky player at the Hawaiian Village.

And in 1899 the *Hawaiian Almanac and Annual* reported: 'The musical instruments peculiar to the islands are the ukulele or taropatch. They are small guitar shaped instruments, made of native woods, hundreds of which are sold to visiting tourists, and are now scattered all over the world.'

The humble *machete* had arrived in Honolulu only twenty years previously. In that short space of time it had not only become Hawaii's national instrument, but it was also poised to charm the world.

This replica of an 1890 Augusto Dias ukulele was made by Duane Heilman of Black Bear Ukuleles.

HULA HULA GIRLS
HAWAIIAN VILLAGE

Uke Hits the Big Time

FOLLOWING ITS DIZZY rise to domination in Hawaii, the humble ukulele went on to conquer the United States. There, believe it or not, the small guitar became sexy, embodying fun and freedom. The process had started in the last few years of the 19th century, after the overthrow of Hawaii's monarchy and the annexation of the islands by the United States. Hawaii's commercial ambitions and the rise of radio were both key factors in the uke's success story, and by the mid-Twenties around four million were being made and sold each year in the USA. We call it the First Wave.

The spread of the ukulele to North America was not an accident. Various well-planned sorties were made by Hawaiian musicians with the express intention of increasing trade. In 1901 the Hawaiian Glee Club, consisting of ten singers backed by violin, flute, saxophone, cello, two guitars and four ukuleles, travelled north to play at such events as the Pan-American Exposition in Buffalo, New York. *Hula* girls or 'female troubadours' danced to the music, and the audience could sample pineapple juice. A group named Toots Paka's Hawaiians also did much to spread word of the uke by touring the major US cities. In 1903 the Honolulu Chamber of Commerce and Merchants Association formed the Hawaii Promotion Committee and started working hard at promoting Hawaii as a tourist destination and investment opportunity. One result of this initiative was that virtuoso ukulele player Ernest Kaai performed at the Alaska-Yukon-Pacific Exposition, a show that proved to 'very noticeably stimulate the pineapple business', according to a report sent back to the Promotion Committee.

The uke craze grew. By 1910 Hawaiian manufacturers, such as Manuel Nunes, Ernest Kaai, Samuel K. Kamaka and the Aloha Ukulele Company were making about 600 ukuleles every month. Kaai demanded that the uke be taken seriously, saying in 1906: 'Some would call the ukulele an insignificant instrument, and yet we have all there that is necessary

Hula girls (top) and a Hawaiian uke player (above) at the Hawaiian Village, Pan-American Exposition in Buffalo, New York, 1901.

to make and cover an accompaniment for the most difficult opera written.'

One important catalyst for the uke boom in the USA was the 1912 Broadway musical *Bird of Paradise* by Richard Tully. It featured Hawaiian music and further boosted the ukulele's popularity. It made over a million dollars in profit. The *New York Times* had no doubt about the effect of the musical on uke sales: 'How many incantatory ukuleles it set to strumming in the national moonlight will never be known, but for better or for worse their source is definite.' Next, songwriters in Tin Pan Alley (New York's music publishing district) started composing pseudo-Hawaiian songs with titles such as the delightful 'Oh How She Could Yacki Hacki Wicki Wacki Woo', and sheet music flew off the shelves.

The uke was particularly popular with Californian women, a phenomenon noted by author Jack London, who had visited Hawaii. His 1913 novel *The Valley of the Moon* describes a

(Above) A Hawaiian quintet in 1905, complete with two ukes.

The uke's popularity was boosted in 1915 by the Panama-Pacific International Exposition in San Francisco (below).

Aeroplane View Main Group of Exhibit Palaces Panama-Pacific International Exposition

Ernest Kaai (1881–1962)

HAWAIIAN UKULELE VIRTUOSO AND COMPOSER

Ernest Kaai is the most important of the early ukulele players. He has been called 'the first major Hawaiian talent agency' as a result of the huge numbers of musicians he hired to play in his many and various bands. In particular, he recorded with the Ernest Kaai Glee Club. He also promoted tours in Hawaii and on the US mainland. He was the first Hawaiian to tour Australia with a troupe of ten dancers and musicians, among them one Miss Anehila, who danced the Maori *haka*.

Kaai also toured regularly in Asia, visiting Japan, Burma, India and China in 1919. Of the importance of the ukulele, he said: 'It is as needful to any Hawaiian quintet club as a snare drum is to a military brass band.'

He was the first Hawaiian music publisher, bringing out *Souvenir Collection of Hawaiian Songs and Views* in 1917. He also wrote the first ukulele handbooks, *The Ukulele: A Hawaiian Guitar* (1916) and *Hawaii: Ukulele Song Classic* (1917), which meticulously described various strokes, such as waltz, syncopation and rag. Indeed, his techniques are still in use today.

Songwriter Johnny Noble called him 'Hawaii's greatest ukulele player'. In 1941 he retired and settled near Miami, where he opened a music shop.

An advertisement for Ernest Kaai's band, the Troubadores, in the *Honolulu Star* newspaper, 1911.

bohemian gathering on the beach, where his heroine Saxon Brown plays the uke: 'The girls lighted on Saxon's ukulele, and nothing would do but she must play and sing. Several of them had been to Honolulu and knew the instrument ... Also, they knew Hawaiian songs ... and soon, to her accompaniment, all were singing "Aloha Oe", "Honolulu Tomboy" and "Sweet Lei Lehua".'

In 1915 US manufacturers started producing cheap ukes, but according to the *New York Times* of 19 September that year:

> *The Hawaiians ... are angry because certain manufacturers of musical instruments in the U.S. are making ukuleles and stamping them with the legend Made in Hawaii. The thing makes a sweet jingle somewhat as fetching as the melody of mandolins.*

Appetite for the uke was fuelled by the Pan-Pacific International Exposition in San Francisco, also in 1915. Visiting the Hawaiian stand

(Above) Sheet music from the Twenties. 'Ukulele Lady' has since been recorded by the likes of Bette Midler, Peter Sellers and Kermit the Frog.

Tin Pan Alley

Tin Pan Alley is the name given to the area of New York where composers, publishers and pluggers of American popular music established themselves in the early part of the 20th century. Between 1900 and 1930, a Hawaiian craze swept through Tin Pan Alley, and its composers churned out dozens of pseudo-Hawaiian songs, with titles such as 'Yacka Hula Dickey Dula', 'My Honolulu Ukulele Baby' and 'They're Wearing 'em Higher in Hawaii'. It was reported that in 1916 more Hawaiian-style records were sold than any other form of music. Some of these songs were smash hits sung by stars such as Al Jolson. A virtuous circle was formed: Tin Pan Alley songwriters were influenced by Hawaiian music, and Hawaiian music was popularized by Tin Pan Alley. Sheet music was also published in vast quantities. Clearly, music in those days was more self-played: the public would buy the music and then play the song at home on the piano, uke or violin. Our favourite song from Tin Pan Alley's Hawaiian period is the incomparable 'Ukulele Lady' by Gus Kahn and Richard Whiting.

at the Expo, musician Irving Fisher comments on the 'fresh-faced, zoftig [buxom] hula girls in their little grass skirts', and goes on to say:

> I was ... more taken by the haunting and yet bouncy sound of a shrunken guitar that I soon learned is called the ukulele. An orchestra of these joyous instruments backs the undulating hula girls and [the] combination of the wobble of sounds with the shaking of hips was intoxicating ... this was the fad of the hour, and I had to catch the wave before it broke and I'd be washed up.

And in 1917 a newspaper report describes the craze:

> Hawaii has captured America. From every phonograph shop come the strains of the Hilo March. The boy in the street whistles 'Hello, Hawaii, How Are You?' Our music teachers have closed the piano and put aside the violin and in order to live they advertise lessons on the ukulele and the Hawaiian guitar.

This period saw an explosion of teach-yourself ukulele manuals, whose cover pictures often featured Western couples in exotic Hawaiian scenes. *The Kamiki Ukulele Method* (1921) is a favourite of ours: on the cover a girl with bobbed hair sweetly strums the uke in a canoe while her dashing lover mans the paddle.

In the egalitarian image on the cover of *The Kamiki Ukulele Method* instruction manual (top right), the girl serenades the man. A similar escape fantasy adorns the cover of the 1920 song 'Dreamy Paradise' (opposite).

The increasing demand for ukuleles in America encouraged many US instrument manufacturers to jump on the bandwagon. The 1915 'Style 2' ukulele (near right) was made by C.F. Martin & Co., while the 1920s 'Style 3' (far right) was made by the Gibson Mandolin-Guitar Mfg. Co. Style numbers indicate the fanciness of a uke. The more decorative inlays and binding on the fretboard and top, the higher the style number.

Ernest Kaai's 1916 guide *The Ukulele: A Hawaiian Guitar* was a landmark publication. It contains the first printed description of the common ukulele stroke: 'Take the down stroke squarely on the nail of the finger and the up stroke with the fleshy part of the finger.' Other notable uke instruction books were written by the virtuoso player Roy Smeck and the uke evangelist May Singhi Breen.

The First Wave of the ukulele was aided enormously by new developments in technology: the instrument had first been recorded by the Edison label in 1899, and now other labels, such as Victor and Columbia, started releasing recordings by native musicians. And radio, of course, had a huge influence. The first station went on the air in 1920, and within two years there were nearly 500 more. Sales of radio sets increased sixfold between 1922 and 1924. Right from the beginning, Hawaiian music and the ukulele were programme staples. 'The radio listener is certain to tune in on some

Sheet music and gramophone records sold in huge quantities during the Twenties.

Hapa Haole

Literally meaning 'half white' in Hawaiian, *hapa haole* has come to describe a musical style that is a hybrid of Hawaiian and non-Hawaiian styles. It can also refer to songs with just a few Hawaiian words among predominantly English lyrics. An example of such a song is 'The Cockeyed Mayor of Kaunakakai', which includes such lines as, 'He wore a *lei* and he wore a smile / He drank a gallon of *oke* to make life worthwhile.' *Hapa haole* songs tend to feature sex and humour: the master of the suggestive lyric was Sonny Cunha, who penned the following lines in 1905: 'She dresses fine, most divine and the Malihines say she's a beauty / O how she loves to dance when in a trance she'll take a chance.' And how about 'My Lu-au Girl' from 1914: 'Some days we drive to the Pali / And make love beneath the trees / And she strums her ukulele / As we sit there in the breeze.'

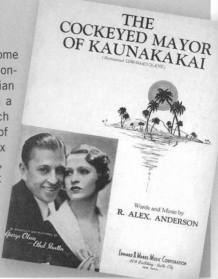

May Singhi Breen (1895–1970)

UKE EVANGELIST

May Singhi Breen is one of the most significant and tireless promoters of the ukulele in its 130-year history. Known as the 'Ukulele Lady', the New Yorker started playing the instrument in 1922, and joined an all-female ukulele group called the Syncopators. She then met songwriter Peter De Rose, whom she later married, and the pair presented their own radio show, *Sweethearts of the Air*, from 1923 to 1936. May played the uke to Peter's piano accompaniment.

Breen taught the ukulele and published method books too. Her great contribution was to go beyond chords, and teach how to play melody on the instrument. Her slogan was the weakly punning 'Uke can play the melody'. In her book *New Ukulele Method* (1950) she says that the ukulele 'should head the list of every recreational program in schools, camps and Girls' and Boys' Clubs in educational centers. Group-playing leads to enjoyment for young and old.'

In addition to her teaching work, she published arrangements of popular songs for the ukulele, and became famous enough for the musical instrument manufacturer P'Mico to bring out a May Singhi Breen signature banjo ukulele.

As a great evangelist for the instrument, Breen liked to emphasize how it lent itself to conviviality: 'I wish I could tell you of the many lasting relationships that have resulted through the medium of the groups, which I had the pleasure of forming and training.'

Roy Smeck (1900–94)

VAUDEVILLE UKE PLAYER

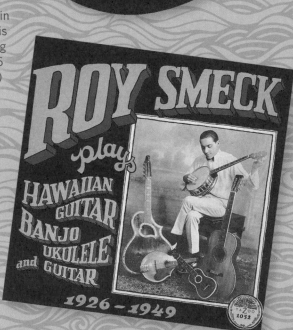

The brilliantined Roy Smeck was a virtuoso ukulele and banjo player with a penchant for music-hall-style tricks. He was a showman who incorporated a range of bizarre antics into his act, including spinning the ukulele, using it as a percussion instrument, playing it upside down, blowing into it and throwing it in the air. All this was performed as he wore his trademark, and slightly sinister, grin. You can see a few of his extraordinary performances on YouTube. He may come over today as a slightly silly novelty act, but his technical wizardry is undeniable.

Smeck quit school at fifteen and got work in a shoe factory, but was fired for practising his uke in the toilets. He was later spotted playing in a music store by a salesman, and by 1926 was earning $250 a week (about $3000 today) playing at the Hamilton Theater in New York. In that year he played the ukulele in one of the first-ever sound films, *Don Juan*, starring John Barrymore. He later hosted his own show on a New York radio station, WOR, and each day would give his listeners a fifteen-minute lesson in a different musical instrument.

Smeck gave his name to a line of signature ukes produced by Chicago's Harmony Company, and millions of these instruments were sold. The pear-shaped Vita-Uke, introduced in 1927, was a particularly big seller, and you can still come across it today. Apart from its distinctive shape, the Vita-Uke also featured sound holes in the shape of performing seals.

Roy Smeck toured the world and even played at George VI's coronation review in 1936. His most notable ukulele album is *The Magic Ukulele of Roy Smeck* (1959). He died at the age of 94.

Roy Smeck had a showy performance style that included 'tapping' and 'windmilling' techniques that would later be adopted by rock guitar legends such as Pete Townshend.

(Left) Detail from the sheet music of the novelty song 'O'Brien Is Tryin' to Learn to Talk Hawaiian'.

(Below) A 'pineapple ukulele' made in Hawaii in the late Twenties by the Kamaka company. The distinctive shape, which produces a mellower sound than the usual figure-eight shape, was designed by Samuel Kamaka, whose grandchildren still run the family company.

ukulele playing somewhere or other before the evening is over,' said the *Los Angeles Times* in 1923. And that year the *New York Times* reported: 'Since the growth of broadcasting, the kindness with which [the radio] treats [the saxophone, banjo and ukulele] has carried the three to a prominence they could never have attained in the same period of time through any other medium.'

In the Twenties the uke's attraction as a solo instrument began to be realized. One catalyst was a 1924 radio programme in Hawaii that featured August Kim playing a ukulele solo.

That decade also saw major stars emerge: uke player Wendell Hall's 1924 song 'It Ain't Gonna Rain No More' hit two million sales, whereupon one newspaper report quipped 'a virulent epidemic of ukulele has broken out', and then extended

Cliff Edwards

Better known as 'Ukulele Ike', Cliff Edwards (1895–1971) was a huge star in the Twenties and did much to popularize the uke. Having cut his teeth on the vaudeville circuit, he played the uke in George Gershwin's 1924 smash hit stage musical *Lady Be Good* starring Fred Astaire, and later sang 'Singin' in the Rain' in the musical movie *The Hollywood Revue* of 1929. His biographer Larry Kiner claims that Edwards sold 74 million records throughout his career. In 1940 he was cast as the voice of Jiminy Cricket in Walt Disney's *Pinocchio*, and sings 'When You Wish Upon a Star'. He also sings 'When I See an Elephant Fly' in *Dumbo* (1941). Sadly, his later years saw him descend into alcoholism.

the metaphor: 'Efforts to check it have proved unsuccessful and physicians say that it will probably run its course far into the winter or at least until "It Ain't Gonna Rain No More".' Other notable performers of the Twenties included Cliff Edwards, aka Ukulele Ike, and vaudeville star Johnny Marvin, who presented his gold-plated signature uke to King Edward VIII in England.

The uke was a must-have for college students, as seen in Harold Lloyd's 1925 film *The Freshman*: the keen young undergraduate hero arrives for his first term clutching the obligatory instrument.

Ukulele clubs thrived in schools across the United States as a means of teaching music to children. 'The work of the numerous ukulele clubs has been recognized as a means towards bringing out latent musical talent and as furnishing a starting point for more serious musical endeavor,' reported the Division of Musical Activities for Los Angeles in 1927.

The ukulele craze hit England too. According to Jessica Mitford in her memoir *Hons and Rebels*, her sister Nancy, a 'bright young thing' given to daring new habits, annoyed her family by taking up the instrument. She recalls: '... Nancy using lipstick, Nancy playing the newly fashionable ukulele, Nancy wearing trousers, Nancy smoking a cigarette.' The novelist Malcolm Lowry (1909–57) was also famously a uke player. In the summer of 1924 the *New York Times* reported that the young Edward Windsor, Prince of Wales, having visited Hawaii, had 'expressed a desire to learn to play the Hawaiian instrument'. By the 1930s he had apparently mastered it, under the tutelage of one Kelvin Keech.

But the delicious optimism of the Twenties, and the uke's popularity, were to fade in the Thirties, as the Depression and then the Second World War loomed on the horizon.

In the Twenties the manufacturer Regal made the charming ukes (above) featuring the popular cartoon character Harold Teen and his bob-haired girlfriend, Lillums Lovewell (below).

(Opposite) Uke fan Prince Edward, Duke of Windsor, goes native on Waikiki Beach, Hawaii, in 1920.

The Uke is Mocked

THE FORTUNES OF THE UKULELE took a spectacular dive around 1930. The small guitar began to be seen as a joke, particularly in the United States. Sales declined, as indicated by the manufacturer Martin's annual production figures. The high point had been in 1926, when over 14,000 ukuleles were sold. By 1933 this figure had dwindled to just 737. Uke expert Jim Beloff blames the big-band craze for the ukulele's decline in popularity, but perhaps its ubiquity meant that people simply got tired of it. The banjolele-playing George Formby was huge in the UK, but still the uke suffered.

Hawaiian imagery and the ukulele became fodder for comedy. In the 1933 film *Sons of the Desert*, Oliver Hardy plays the uke and sings 'Honolulu Baby' alongside a pineapple-wielding Stan Laurel.

Do we detect a hint of mockery in Laurel and Hardy's adoption of pineapple, *lei* and ukulele (below)?

(Opposite) Cliff Edwards, aka Ukulele Ike, in 1930, when the uke's popularity in the USA was starting to decline.

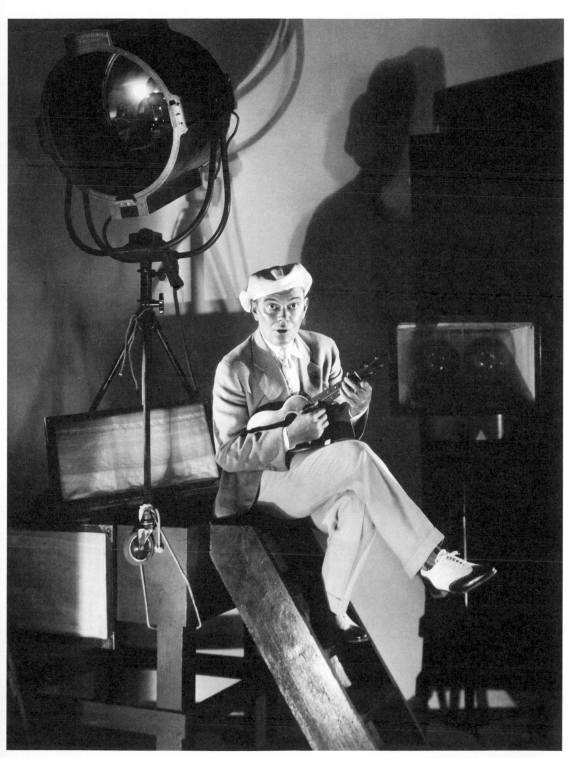

In P.G. Wodehouse's 1934 novel *Thank You, Jeeves* the banjo ukulele, commonly called the banjolele, is mocked as a 'hideous musical instrument'.

Gracie Allen played the uke during a song and dance number on the deck of a Hawaii-bound cruise ship in the movie *Honolulu* (1939). The ukulele also appeared in publicity stills for comedies such as *Waikiki Wedding* (1939) starring Bing Crosby, and for *The Road to Singapore* (1940), although not in the movies themselves.

The ukulele is teased in *Thank You, Jeeves* by P.G. Wodehouse (1934). Bertie Wooster takes up the banjolele, and infuriates Jeeves with his practising. The valet actually gives notice rather than listen to Bertie playing the hot tunes of the day, such as 'I Want an Automobile with a Horn That Goes Toot-Toot'. Neither is Sir Roderick Glossop, uncle of Bertie's pal Tuppy, pleased about the new hobby: 'For weeks, it appears, you have been making life hell for all your neighbours with some hideous musical instrument. I see you have it with you now. How dare you play that thing in a respectable block of flats? Infernal din!'

Mocking the uke was not altogether a new sport: in 1923 the theft of five ukuleles from a freight car was reported. In court the judge took the opportunity to attack the ukulele rather than the felon: 'I am tempted to give you my address instead of sending you to prison,' he quipped. 'In the house next to mine there is a young man who plays one of these instruments.' Journalists also scoffed: 'They say that for many years no one knew who invented the ukulele,' wrote a columnist in the *Los Angeles Times* in 1927. 'At last the offender, conscience-stricken, surrendered himself to the authorities and was duly hanged.' We are reminded of the joke: 'A gentleman is a man who knows how to the play the ukulele – but doesn't.' Worse still, a ukulele string is used to strangle a beautiful young woman in Agatha Christie's short story 'The Bird with the Broken Wing' (1930).

The ukulele's fortunes continued to decline. In a 1932 report America's National Recreation Association called the ukulele 'inferior' and 'low grade', and in 1936 the *Christian Science Monitor* asked of the uke: 'Where is the instrument today? One scarcely hears it, even on Major Bowe's or Fred Allen's amateur hours ... the "uke" apparently is going rapidly into the limbo of the mandolin.'

An attempt by the industry to boost sales in 1937 with National Ukulele Week was a failure. Even the big ukulele stars distanced themselves from the instrument. In 1930 Ukulele Ike told a newspaper that he wanted to get rid of the ukulele and was no longer 'merely a song and dance man'. Wendell Hall continued to appear on the radio, but rarely with his uke; and Johnny Marvin, who had been a massive star, was reduced to scrabbling around for flat-fee session work.

Hawaiian music even suffered a decline in Hawaii itself. The biggest name there in ukulele during this period was Jesse Kalima (1920–1980). He developed the ukulele as a solo instrument and

Martin Ukuleles

American guitar manufacturer C.F. Martin & Co. of Pennsylvania, founded in 1833, entered the ukulele market in 1916, and rode the uke boom of the Twenties. They made fine ukuleles of mahogany and Hawaiian koa wood, and produced a number of different models labelled from zero to five – the higher the number, the fancier the uke. Model 0, for example, was described as 'plain, neat, serviceable' in their 1940 catalogue, while styles 3 and 5 offered ebony fingerboards and pretty pearl inlay position marks. The letter 'K' after a model number indicated ukes made from Hawaiian koa wood. The 5K is considered by collectors to be the ultimate jewel in the crown, and a vintage model would today set you back $10,000. In 1924 it was priced at $55. The highest sales figures were achieved in 1926, when 14,101 Martin ukes were sold, and in 1950, when the figure reached 11,722. Demand fell sharply during the Sixties, and production stopped completely in the Seventies. Now the Martin company has re-entered the uke market, and offers a range of fourteen styles, using mahogany and koa. 'The OXK uke is perfect for moonlight serenading on the beach,' says the catalogue of its most inexpensive model. And the 5K is back too, priced at a mere five grand, a sure sign that today's ukulele boom is real.

The movie *Hawaii Calls* (1938) – with Bobby Breen, left, and Ned Sparks, right – was named after the weekly US radio show promoting the islands. But all things Hawaiian lost their appeal during the late Thirties and throughout the Forties.

released a number of 78s during this period. But Kalima and Eddie Kamae, the other great player of the time, did not play Hawaiian music on the instrument, preferring instead to perform pieces such as Ravel's *Bolero*, American marches and Latin rhythms.

Hawaii's tourism industry had been hit by the Depression, and music was used as a tool to revive it. In 1935 the Hawaii Tourist Bureau launched a weekly radio show, *Hawaii Calls*, which lasted for 40 years and promoted the islands as a laid-back paradise. The PR effort was a partial success: in the US Hawaiian clubs and tiki (cocktail) bars opened up, such as Don the Beachcomber in LA and Trader Vic's in Oakland, California. In 1937 Paramount released the Hawaii-based Bing Crosby movie *Waikiki Wedding*, which produced 'Sweet Leilani', the Oscar-winning hit by Harry Owens. It was one of the biggest-grossing films of the year, but it still failed to revive the uke's fortunes.

George Formby (1904–61)
SUPERSTAR OF THE THIRTIES

More than anyone else in Britain, George Formby is associated with the ukulele. And although he is acknowledged to be a fine strummer, it has taken many years for the uke to shake off the comical reputation that he gave to it. Formby was the fourth child of a popular northern entertainer, also called George Formby. Formby Senior (originally called James Booth) was the illegitimate son of a notorious Lancashire prostitute named Sarah Jane Booth, who in a ten-year period was convicted 140 times for drunkenness, theft, vagrancy and brawling. Frequently beaten by his mother's various partners, James had an absolutely miserable childhood. At the age of twelve he went to work in a cotton mill, but started singing at pubs in the evenings. When he was nineteen, the manager of the Argyle Theatre in Birkenhead suggested the name change: George after the famous comedian George Robey, and Formby after a small town whose name he'd spotted on coal wagons.

Formby Senior became a wealthy man, commanding as much as £50 an appearance – over £4000 in today's money. Formby Junior, George Hoy Booth, was born on 26 May 1904, and his father did his best to keep him away from the stage. In 1911 he was sent to work at a riding stables, where he was to train as a jockey. Nonetheless, he did act in a 1915 movie called *By the Shortest of Heads*, but Formby Senior hoped that this foray into showbiz was a one-off, when the boy went to work at a stable in Ireland. There he was bullied and made frequent attempts to run away. In 1921 his father died aged just 45.

With his mother Eliza's help, George launched himself onto the stage. He spent two years touring northern halls as 'George Hoy, son of George Formby', performing songs from his father's act. In 1923 he acquired his first banjo ukulele or 'banjolele'. He incorporated it into his act, told parrot jokes, and immediately received standing ovations. Later in the year he met a clog-dancer called Beryl Ingham. He fell for her and they were married on 13 September 1924.

Formby's biographers have no doubt that the bossy, domineering Beryl, who acted as Formby's business manager, was a major force behind his success. But they say that she also made him unhappy by, for example, never having sex with him. She mothered him: 'If I leave George alone for a minute he goes off and buys a new car or a new jumper.'

Formby put on successful shows during the Twenties, and he started making records, notably 'Chinese Laundry Blues' by Jack Cottrell, recorded in 1932. It concerns the doings of a Mr Wu, and here is a typical couplet: 'Now Mr Wu, he's got a naughty eye that flickers / You ought to see it wobble when he's ironing ladies' blouses.'

The next release was 'I Told My Baby with My Ukulele', written by Harry Gifford and Fred E. Cliffe, on Decca. This song was sadly withdrawn following complaints about its obvious substitution of the word 'ukulele' for penis: 'Come on, big boy, get busy! / But I kept my ukulele in my hand!'

George's first proper movie role was in a love story called *Boots, Boots* (1934), which was a hit in the north, though not in the West End, and more followed. In 1936 he recorded 'When I'm Cleaning Windows', another innuendo-laden ditty from Gifford and Cliffe. It sold 150,000 copies in a month, but was banned by the BBC. Puritanical BBC controller John Reith said at the time: 'If the public wants to listen to Formby singing his disgusting little ditty, they'll have to be content to hear it in the cinemas, not over the nation's airwaves.' An appalled Beryl marched into Reith's office to complain, and he read out an apology over the airwaves, although he did not lift to the ban.

By 1939 Formby had become Britain's best-paid entertainer, earning £100,000 a year, which would be nearly £5 million today. However, meanie Beryl allowed him only five shillings a day pocket money. The couple never had children, but they both had affairs: Beryl with film star Gavin Gordon, and George with his leading ladies. But the girls often found George boring. One co-star, Phyllis Calvert, said of him: 'He was a very dull man.'

In 1940 George went off to entertain the troops, playing to 40,000 soldiers in Brittany. In 1941 he performed for George VI and Elizabeth, who requested

(Above) George and Beryl Formby in 1934.

(Opposite) Entertaining troops in 1939 at a seaside concert hall in northern England.

the uncensored version of 'When I'm Cleaning Windows'. They were delighted by it, presenting George with gold cufflinks, and Beryl with a silver powder-compact.

The Formbys visited the Holy Land in 1943, playing shows at a base near Tel Aviv and in Egypt. Beryl's toughness had a courageous and noble side, as she showed on a visit to South Africa in October 1946. The Formbys, having played to thousands of fans, were invited to lunch in Pretoria with Daniel François Malan, head of the National Party, who would introduce apartheid in 1948. Malan had warned the Formbys that they would not be allowed to perform to black audiences. Beryl said at the time: 'If that man turns up at the do, George and I will be on the first plane back to England.' He didn't turn up, and Beryl went on to antagonize him further by arranging to play gigs to black-only audiences, where

George in discussion with the bandleader-cum-spy Garry Marsh in the 1940 film *To Hell with Hitler*, which is generally regarded as Formby's best movie.

entry was free of charge. They hugged the children, handed out sweets and chatted to the parents. Malan called her in a fury and she said to him: 'Why don't you piss off, you horrible little man?'

Malan's office told the Formbys that they would have to leave at once. As they boarded the plane, a message came through from Malan: 'Never come here again!' On a second trip to South Africa in 1955 (Malan having resigned), Beryl told journalists: 'All this racial stuff is just rubbish. We're all the same colour inside, so why pick on people just because they're a different colour on the outside? Black, white or sky-blue pink with yellow dots on, they're just as good as you!'

For George the Fifties were marred by ill health. He suffered from dysentery and depression, and more than once announced his retirement. Meanwhile, Beryl fell ill with cancer of the uterus, and the two took to heavy drinking, generally while on cruise ships. George fell in love with Pat Howson, the 29-year-old daughter of a family friend, and also had an affair with the gorgeous singer Yana, who appeared with him on the bill at a Blackpool revue. Throughout this time he grew more ill; in particular his lungs were shot thanks to smoking 40 cigarettes a day since the age of twelve.

In December 1960 Beryl died and not a single showbiz connection showed up at her funeral. The following year George became engaged to Pat Howson. He died in March 1961, at the age of 57, two days before he was due to be married.

The ukulele fared a little better in the UK thanks to that grinning master of the double entendre, George Formby. Playing comic songs to the accompaniment of his banjo ukulele, which he strummed with great rhythmic virtuosity, he appeared in 21 movies. By 1939 he was earning £100,000 a year, making him by far the best-paid entertainer in the UK of his day. His biographer John Fisher wrote: 'There can hardly have been a single moment of any day from 1935 until the end of the war when the voice of George Formby was not heard somewhere in England.' But much as we love and admire George, his popularity has probably contributed to the perception, still held by some, that the ukulele is a mere toy or novelty instrument, a prop for a comedy act.

Hawaiian music did not vanish entirely in the UK during the Thirties and Forties. A Hawaiian group called the Royal Hawaiians played at London's Café Anglais in 1930, and then British musicians caught the bug and studied steel guitar and ukulele. Among the biggest names were the Hawaiian Islanders, a group of Brits, also

Japanese-American soldiers amuse themselves with a Kamale ukulele as they await to detrain at Camp Shelby, Mississippi, in 1943.

A.P. SHARPE'S HONOLULU HAWAIIANS

Stars of the UK Hawaiian music scene in 1930s included A.P. Sharpe's Honolulu Hawaiians (left) and the Hawaiian Islanders (below), featuring Joe Hodgkinson on the ukulele (below left).

Best Wishes
Joe Hodgkin.
1934

known as the Hodgkinson Brothers. With Joe Hodgkinson (who died in 2009, aged 90) on the ukulele, they specialized in authentic Hawaiian songs and played in West End clubs. The war put an end to the group, which played its last gig in 1940.

The Thirties and Forties also saw other British groups playing exotic music: these included the Coral Islanders, Kealoha Life and His Island Music, and Patrick Forbes' South Sea Islanders. A.P. Sharpe's Honolulu Hawaiians played at Butlins and made 400 broadcasts for the radio. The *aloha* dream persisted despite the decline of the uke.

Having been popular in Japan in the Thirties, the ukulele's fortunes took a dive there as well. From 1937 to 1944 the authorities cracked down on Hawaiian music on the grounds, according to *Hawaiian Music and Musicians*, that the steel guitar and banjo 'weakened the young people's will' with their 'foggy, murky tone'. The ukulele was seen as a subversive influence and disappeared.

The decline in the ukulele's fortunes mirrored a general collapse in the record industry. In 1921 Americans had bought 110 million records, but in 1933 that figure had dropped to 10 million. Historians blame the jukebox, which let people listen to their favourite tunes in public places very cheaply, so there was no need to buy the records.

Come 1949, though, the uke would hit the big time once again, thanks to two hot new technologies: television and plastic.

The Uke Goes Plastic

IN 1948 THE VICE president of musical instrument manufacturer Gretsch pronounced of the ukulele: 'Its popularity today is practically nil. I can honestly say it is deader than a doornail.' The Forties had not been kind to the uke; sales had dwindled to almost nothing.

But reports of the ukulele's death were exaggerated. At that very point, against all expectations, the small guitar sprang back to life. According to the *New York Times* in the summer of 1949: 'The ukulele and banjo are making a strong comeback ... interest in the two strummed instruments is greater now than at any time since the Twenties.' That year's hit Rodgers and Hammerstein musical, *South Pacific*, with its Hawaiian vibe, probably contributed to renewed interest in the uke, and postwar optimism may have been another factor.

But the real force behind the Fifties' ukulele boom came from the convergence of two new technologies: television and plastic. Add one outstanding man, TV and radio star and uke evangelist Arthur Godfrey (1903–1983), and the conditions were set for a mighty uke renaissance. We call it the Second Wave.

The growth of television in the US was phenomenal: in 1948 just 350,000 American households had a TV; by 1952, that figure had reached 15.3 million. At the same time, wartime research, paid for by the government during the Second World War, had led to great leaps forward in the field of synthetic polymers. 'Everything's gonna be made out of plastic,' Woody Guthrie had predicted in 1941, and so it was to be. The first plastic ukulele, Mattel's Uke-a-Doodle, was launched in January 1947. A rival called the Uke-a-Tune was released later in the year by American

Arthur Godfrey (top), king of the Fifties' airwaves and promoter of the ukulele.

Mattel's Uke-a-Doodle plastic instruments (above) were launched in 1947.

The Islander ukulele (left), as promoted on TV by Arthur Godfrey, complete with Emenee's 'Arthur Godfrey Uke Player' (above), a device that automatically formed a chord at the press of a button.

Plastic Products. It was successfully targeted at children, whom uke experts reckon made up 80 per cent of the market in the Fifties.

The laid-back Arthur Godfrey was the undisputed king of American radio and TV in the late Forties and early Fifties. He hit the big time with his show for CBS Radio, *Arthur Godfrey's Talent Scouts*, which was the *X-Factor* of its day, launching stars such as Tony Bennett, Patsy Cline and Lenny Bruce, while a young singer called Elvis Presley was rejected. The show was later broadcast simultaneously on radio and TV, as was his morning show, *Arthur Godfrey Time*. Godfrey even gave lessons to the nation on another TV show, *Arthur Godfrey and His Ukulele*, which ran for three months in 1950. At his peak, Godfrey reached 40 million viewers and listeners every week, and his shows brought in $10 million a year in advertising revenue to CBS.

Godfrey played a key role in the creation of the plastic ukulele. In 1947 he teamed up with musician and manufacturer Mario Maccaferri, an Italian who had fled Europe in 1939. Maccaferri was struggling financially owing to an unlucky speculation in plastic clothes spinners. But, following a meeting with Godfrey, he developed a good-quality plastic ukulele, the Islander, based on Martin's Model 0 (see page 39). It was priced at $5.95 (around $55 today). Given mass production technology, Maccaferri reckoned he could produce 26,000 ukuleles a day. Godfrey went on to plug the plastic instrument on his TV show, and by the end of 1950, Maccaferri's company, Mastro Industries, had sold 350,000 ukuleles. A newspaper in Massachusetts reported: 'Local musical instrument dealers have been unable to satisfy the demand here, especially since a New York man tossed his plastic uke on the market to supplement the wooden variety, admirably timed to the TV pulse of Mrs Godfrey's big fat boy, Arthur.' Other manufacturers also benefited: Gretsch, whose vice president had so recently pronounced the uke dead, were producing 1000 a week, and by August 1950 national uke sales in the US had reached 1.7 million. In total, 9 million Mastro plastic ukuleles were sold, though the company went on to make various other ukes, including the Sparkle Plenty Islander Ukette, the Islander Baritone Ukulele and a banjolele. The instruments were often packaged with a biography of Arthur Godfrey, and a songbook and playing guide by May Singhi Breen.

The competition in the plastic uke market became fierce. Toy giant Emenee weighed in with a copy of the Islander called the Flamingo, and although the sound quality was inferior, it achieved excellent sales. In addition, they signed a contract

Mastro's TV Pal ukulele (left).

Sparkle Plenty's Islander Ukette (below left), Mastro's uke for kids.

Emenee's Flamingo ukulele (below), a rival to the Islander.

A huge variety of plastic ukes
was produced during the Fifties
and sold in jaunty, colourful
packaging. These examples are
from the collection of Antoine
Carolus, aka UkeHeidi.

with Arthur Godfrey, causing Mastro's sales to take a tumble.

High-quality ukuleles also sold well: in 1950 Martin's ukulele sales reached 11,722, its highest figure since 1926, when over 14,000 were sold.

As in the Twenties, uke manuals flew off the shelves. Arthur Godfrey penned the foreword to a 1950 instruction manual called *You can Play the Ukulele* by Don Ball, an executive at CBS. 'There just isn't any greater ukulele player in the whole United States than Don Ball!' gushed Godfrey. And Don Ball writes in the book: 'Today, thanks largely to radio and television promotion by that rambunctious red-head Arthur Godfrey, the uke is more popular than ever!' For Godfrey the uke had a social purpose: 'If a kid has a uke in his hand, he's not going to get in much trouble.'

Thanks to Godfrey and the uke revival, old stars of the Twenties, such as Wendell Hall, Cliff Edwards and Roy Smeck, enjoyed comebacks. Music historians suggest that the US, during a period of Cold War paranoia and nuclear anxiety, craved musical comfort and nostalgia, and that they found it in the form of the uke.

Ukulele method books (above) flew off the shelves during the Second Wave of uke popularity in the Fifties.

The charming comic character Sparkle Plenty (below) finds an appreciative audience for her ukulele playing.

Eddie Kamae (1927–)

HAWAIIAN MUSICIAN WHO PROMOTES THE OLD WAYS

Eddie Kamae's lifelong love affair with the ukulele began at the age of fifteen, when his older brother, a bus driver, found a uke on the back seat of the bus and gave it to Eddie. He started playing while making extra cash by running a dice game at school. At eighteen he joined the army for two years. In 1948 he met another ukulele player, Shoi Ikemi, at Charlie's Cab Stand, an open shed near Iolani Palace, which was used as a sort of open-mike spot every Saturday afternoon. The two formed the Ukulele Rascals and, influenced by jazz guitar legend Django Reinhardt and Latin rhythms, developed an act that really moved the ukulele forward as a serious instrument. Eddie developed a playing style that combined picking and chording, and the pair played Hoagy Carmichael and Ravel rather than traditional Hawaiian music.

The Rascals joined a variety tour and played all over the US, but the touring life was hard, and when Eddie returned to Hawaii, he found an easier way to pay the bills: gambling and crime. He ran dice games at illegal cockfights, and then got himself involved in a scam to pass off cornflour as a household medicine. At 27 he was caught and sentenced to three years in jail. 'I didn't know how I was going to last three years in there,' he later said. 'My uke was my companion and my way to find some peace of mind.'

AN ISLAND HERITAGE P PANINI PRODUCTION
THE FOLK MUSIC OF HAWAII IN BOOK AND RECORD
SONS OF HAWAII
EDDIE KAMAE
JOE MARSHALL
GABBY PAHINUI
MOE KEALE
DAVID ROGERS
STEREO

When this album was released in 1971, Eddie Kamae and the other three original members of Sons of Hawaii were joined by ukulele master Moe Keale, who was the uncle of Israel Kamakawiwo'ole (see page 63).

On his release he played nightly at the Biltmore Hotel in Waikiki. At this stage he was still playing Western music, but that changed when he met the brilliant but unpredictable Gabby Pahinui in the late Fifties. Gabby was a Hawaiian legend who played 'slack key' guitar and held weekend-long jam sessions at his house. It was at one of these parties that Eddie learned to play 'Ku'u Pua I Paokalani' (My Flower at Paokalani), a song written by Queen Lili'uokalani while under house arrest in 1893, which kindled what was to be a lasting love affair with Hawaiian music.

The two men started to play music together regularly. 'We'd wake up at five in the morning, go out in the yard or to the beach and just play all day. We'd have a few beers, sit back and play till it got dark.' They were joined by bassist Joe Marshall and steel guitar player David Rogers, known as 'Feet', and the new band put on their first gig in the spring of 1960. This was the beginning of the movement that became known as the Hawaiian Cultural Renaissance.

Eddie's band was named the Sons of Hawaii, and through the Sixties and Seventies they released several albums that celebrated the traditions of the islands. Meanwhile, Eddie spent lots of time with Hawaiian elders, researching the country's language and customs. He also travelled to the smaller islands of Hawaii, and met the old songwriters in the hills — men such as 90-year-old Sam Li'a, and old cowboy Luther Makekau.

Eddie went on to make many award-winning documentaries, including *Listen to the Forest* (1991) and *Hawaiian Voices: Bringing Past to Present* (1999), which celebrate Hawaii's traditions and songs.

Hawaiian uke legend Eddie Kamae has done much to reconnect Hawaiians with their own history and culture.

When Mario Met Arthur

The Fifties uke boom began with a 1947 meeting between legendary guitar-maker Mario Maccaferri and TV star Arthur Godfrey. 'When are you going to stop playing that silly instrument there?' Maccaferri said to Godfrey. 'Out of this, you cannot get music.' Godfrey replied: 'You can't say that, because the ukulele is such a [great] instrument that no youngster can go bad playing it.' Godfrey told Maccaferri that if he could design a plastic ukulele, they would sell a million. Mario duly invented the Islander and Godfrey plugged it on air: 'Say, you know what? I had a long session with this fellow who makes plastic ukuleles and he's got a lulu of a ukulele. It frets beautifully and has a nice little tone to it – and you can get that, with a couple of picks and an extra set of strings, plus a little book of instructions – the whole deal for $5.95. How about that?' The public went mad for it and millions were indeed sold.

This very rare Regal 'Jungle Uke' was made in Chicago around 1950, and covered in faux leopard skin.

The uke returned to the classroom in the Fifties, and introduced baby boomer stars to music, including Jimi Hendrix, Bob Seger and John Paul Jones. In the early Fifties Neil Young was to be heard playing chords on his uke in his bedroom, and Joan Baez made her first public ukulele performance at a high school talent show, aged fourteen.

Meanwhile, in Hawaii, a duo called the Ukulele Rascals brought the uke centre stage. Eddie Kamae and Shoi Ikemi played their first gig at the Lau Lee Chai restaurant in Waikiki in 1948, becoming the first-ever all-ukulele act. The great uke player Herb Ohta credits the Rascals with hugely boosting the instrument's popularity. They played American songs and classical compositions rather than Hawaiian music, and also introduced tango and rumba rhythms, Mexican *mariachi* techniques, and brought out new subtleties in the instrument. Another great uke player of the Fifties was the Californian Lyle Ritz, whose jazzy playing, to be heard on his 1957 LP *How About Uke?*, took the ukulele to new levels of sophistication.

In Britain Hawaiian music and the uke did not fare so well. In 1955 a new Head of Light Music at the BBC disliked the Hawaiian sound and pulled the plug on broadcasts by A.P. Sharpe's Honolulu Hawaiians. There was only really one outstanding British uke player in the Fifties, and that was variety star Billy 'Uke' Scott, who played a wooden ukulele and appeared on radio shows such as *Workers' Playtime*. He performed comic songs, such as 'A Nice Prefabricated Home', and would end his act with a solo arrangement of 'Ladies of Spain' or 'The William Tell Overture'. The actor Peter Sellers paid tribute to him on a *Goon Show* in 1954. This was not Sellers' only flirtation with the ukulele: in 1960 he recorded a very funny version of the 1925 classic 'Ukulele Lady', with backing from the Temperance Seven. The record was produced by none other than the Beatles' own George Martin.

Following the armistice in 1945, Japan's love affair with Hawaii – dubbed 'the island one dreams about' – was rekindled. New Hawaiian-style groups were formed, notably Poss Miyazaki and his Coney Islanders, and a new style developed that musicologists call Japanese–Hawaiian music.

A compilation of it, entitled *Hawaii Calls*, was released in 1958 by Toshiba Records, and included the hit song 'Kaimana Hila'. Hawaiian music became known as 'summer music' because the records sold only during the summer months. During the Fifties, Hawaiian bands toured the country, and Japan's own Hawaiian-influenced bands played anywhere they could, from rooftops to the newly popular music tearooms.

Marilyn plays the uke in *Some Like It Hot* (1959) while Jack Lemmon and Tony Curtis look on admiringly.

The Beatles (bottom) played on the *Ed Sullivan Show* in 1964. They shared the bill with banjolele artiste Tessie O'Shea (below). Despite plastic ukulele manufacturer Maccaferri's best efforts to cash in on Beatlemania (left), the ukulele looked behind the times.

In Hollywood the ukulele made two notable appearances: the first was in Billy Wilder's *Some Like It Hot* (1959), where Marilyn Monroe sings 'Runnin' Wild' while strumming a uke; and the second was *Blue Hawaii* (1961) starring a 26-year-old Elvis Presley, who was pictured wearing a Hawaiian shirt and playing a uke on posters for the film. The movie stayed at the number one spot for twenty weeks. There was even an Elvis signature uke.

As the Sixties progressed, the ukulele looked increasingly out of date and silly, and the electric guitar, especially in the hands of the Beatles, took centre stage. On 9 February 1964 they played 'She Loves You' and 'I Saw Her Standing There' live to 74 million viewers on the *Ed Sullivan Show*. In between these two songs, an old-style music hall artist named Tessie O'Shea played her banjolele. She looked ridiculous. Overnight, the uke had become hopelessly uncool.

The Uke Goes Underground

IN THE SIXTIES AND SEVENTIES the ukulele all but vanished. In 1968 Martin sold a mere 75 ukes, its lowest total since production began in 1916.

This is not to say that the small guitar disappeared completely. There were a few brave souls who stuck with it.

From 1962 to 1985 a Canadian teacher called J. Chalmers Doane promoted the ukulele as the ideal instrument for teaching children music. He travelled widely, spreading the word to other teachers, published a ukulele manual, produced a special teaching uke, and ran a magazine called *Ukulele Yes!* His protégé James Hill is one of the most exciting uke players in the world today.

In 1968 the strange figure of Tiny Tim appeared on the American TV series *Rowan and Martin's Laugh-In*. He strummed a uke and sang the 1929 song 'Tiptoe Through the Tulips' in falsetto voice. In this context the ukulele was seen by some as a novelty instrument, or even a joke, and for many the association of this peculiar man with the uke was fatal to its credibility.

Another singer, British-born Ian Whitcomb, bravely stuck with his ukulele during the age of rock. A well-educated public schoolboy (born in

Ian Whitcomb (above) was one of the very few uke players of the Sixties. 'I was reviving the ukulele in the era of rock'n'roll, but doing it in a straight and unfreaky way.'

The Northern JCD2 uke (left) was created by Canadian ukulele educator J. Chalmers Doane in the Seventies for use in the classroom.

Tiny Tim (1933–96)

THE WEIRDEST UKE PLAYER EVER

Born Herbert Buckingham Khaury, the son of a Jewish mother and a Catholic father, Tiny Tim grew up in New York City. He was inspired by Arthur Godfrey, from whose classic uke primer *You Too Can Play the Ukulele* he learned his chords. Tim went on to play in Greenwich Village clubs, performing songs from the Tin Pan Alley era in his falsetto voice. In 1968 he appeared on *Rowan and Martin's Laugh-In*, singing 'A Tisket, a Tasket' and 'The Good Ship Lollipop'. Later that year he released his first LP, *God Bless Tiny Tim*, which featured his hit 'Tiptoe Through the Tulips'. *Life* magazine called the record 'one of the most dazzling albums of programmed entertainment to come along since … *Sergeant Pepper*'. Tim became a regular on *Laugh-In* and other prime-time TV programmes, such as Johnny Carson's *Tonight Show*. His televised wedding to Miss Vicki in December

1969 was watched by over 20 million viewers. He would later play 'amusing' cover versions of any song he fancied. In 1996 he made a cameo appearance on *Roseanne*, when he gives Johnny Galeckie a uke lesson. John Goodman walks in and smashes both ukuleles. Tim says: 'That happens to me a lot.' A devout Christian, during an interview with 'shock-jock' Howard Stern, he accused the DJ of taking the name of Jesus in vain. Tiny Tim was a vaudeville entertainer of the old school, and undoubtedly inspired many to take up the uke, but his weirdness rubbed off on the small guitar, and contributed to its reputation as a mere novelty instrument.

(Below) Tiny Tim was married to Miss Vicki Budinger on *The Tonight Show Starring Johnny Carson* in 1969. It looks like the bride enjoyed his song, even if the other guests didn't.

1941), he, like Tiny Tim, was a Tin Pan Alley fan. He was also part of a briefly hip Sixties movement known as the New Vaudeville, led by the Bonzo Dog Doo Da Band and the Jim Kweskin Jug Band (who played a nice version of 'Ukulele Lady' on their 1965 LP). Following a number eight hit in the Billboard charts in 1965 with 'You Turn Me On', he played the ukulele on the TV show *Where the Action Is* in 1966, and recorded a spirited uke version of the Beatles' 'You Won't See Me'. Whitcomb promotes the ukulele to this day and has written a great series of songbooks for Mel Bay Publications, including *Uke Ballads* (2001) and *Ukulele Heaven* (2000).

It is strange to note that the Beatles, the band often credited with killing the uke, actually loved it. George Harrison in particular was a ukulele fan, and played a mean Formby-style split stroke, as evidenced on a clip from *The Beatles Anthology*, where George, Paul and Ringo together sing 'Ain't She Sweet'. Paul also played a jaunty version of 'Something' to ukulele accompaniment at a 2008 show in Liverpool, where he told the audience: 'I'm not sure how many people know it, but George was a really good ukulele player.' He then

The 1971 compilation album *Guava Jam* (below) showcased Hawaiian music during an era when it had few fans.

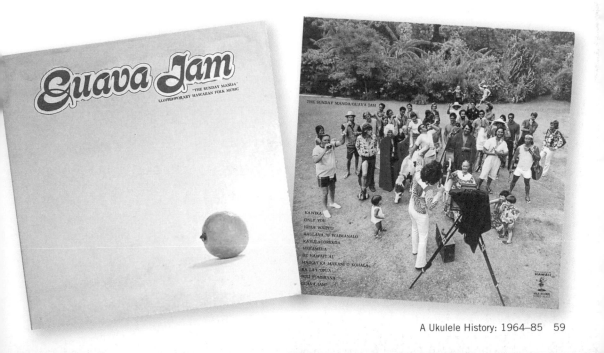

Herb Ohta (top) at the 39th Annual Ukulele Festival in Waikiki, Oahu, Hawaii, 2009.

Ohta's 1964 hit 'Sushi' (above).

revealed that George was a member of the George Formby Society and would visit Blackpool to play along with other members. Nonetheless, the Beatles did not publicly play the uke.

Even in Hawaii the uke suffered a major decline during the Sixties. The exception was the great ukulele virtuoso Herb Ohta, who hit the charts in 1964 with his song 'Sushi' and signed a deal with Decca. Ohta continued to explore the potential of the uke: 'It has the range of the flute, but it can also be chorded,' he said in an interview with the *New York Times* in 1966. However, Ohta had a 1964 US tour cancelled because, he was told, 'the Beatles were coming'. Ohta was a big star in Japan, where he has released 30 albums, and is known as Ohta-san. His easy-listening instrumental 'Song for Anna', released by A&M in 1973, is among the biggest-selling ukulele songs of all time. His album of that title sold six million copies.

Ohta apart, by 1971 both the ukulele and Hawaiian music appeared to have died completely: 'Few people, after all, care to listen to Hawaiian music today; it is now *passé*,' said historian George Kanahele. 'Ask any kid in Hawaii and he will say that Hawaiian music is a drag – it's out, it's dead.' That same year a few activists decided that something should be done. An annual ukulele festival was launched, and Kanahele helped to create the Hawaiian Music Foundation. Also in that year an album called *Guava Jam: Contemporary Hawaiian Folk Music* by Sunday Manoa was released. The standout song is 'Pualilia' with a great uke solo from Peter Moon.

Eddie Kamae (see page 52) also continued to promote traditional Hawaiian music, but the Third Wave of popularity would not really kick off until the early Nineties, when young uke players, such as Israel Kamakawiwo'ole, Kelly Boy Delima and Troy Fernandez, appeared on the scene.

The Uke Returns

THE WORLD is now undeniably in the middle of a giant Third Wave of ukulele popularity. It's a joyful, merry revolution, partially fuelled by the Internet, which has enabled ukulele players all over the world to share their knowledge, expertise and enthusiasm. There are hundreds of ukulele sites, and plenty of characters who are willing to give free online tutorials on the instrument. Also, ukulele bands and clubs are springing up all over the world. The popularity is truly heart-warming because the uke is a genuinely democratic instrument: it is all about sharing rather than showing off, though of course there are some sensational players out there. To boot, the uke suits both genders and all ages.

We can trace the beginnings of the Third Wave, in Britain at least, back to 1985. That was the year musicologist George Hinchliffe formed the delightful Ukulele Orchestra of Great Britain. Comprising six or seven ukes and a bassist, it plays witty and accomplished cover versions of

When formed in the Eighties the Ukulele Orchestra of Great Britain (above) helped stimulate the Third Wave of ukulele popularity in Britain and beyond. Today's line-up (below) keeps the orchestra going strong, touring the world and giving sell-out concerts.

Uke player Troy Fernandez (above right) was among those Hawaiians who revitalized island youth interest in the ukulele. His band, the Ka'au Crater Boys, was hugely popular in the 1990s.

pop songs (George Formby songs are banned, which is a relief to some). Hinchliffe says that the early impetus for the band was not novelty or comedy; it was actually musical: 'We wanted to play a wide variety of music, and the ukulele was perfect as it is so versatile.' The orchestra patiently built up fans all over the world, and a 1994 tour to historically uke-friendly Japan resulted in a new boom over there. Today the 'Ukes', as they are known, can sell out London's Royal Albert Hall, and also have the time to pursue a number of side projects, including operas and collaborations with Ibiza DJs. The ukulele has brought them all a life of freedom.

The Ukes have also spawned hundreds of other ukulele orchestras around the world. 'I see new ones starting nearly every day,' says Hinchliffe. One example is the Ukulele Orchestra of Brno in the Czech Republic, an eight-strong band who play cover versions.

In Hawaii too the ukulele was starting to shake off its image problem. Formerly, young people had rejected the uke and Hawaiian music generally as symbols of cheap tourism, and you have to take their point: listening to Bing Crosby sing 'Blue Hawaii' makes one feel physically sick. But thanks to players such as Israel Kamakawiwo'ole, the ultimate Hawaiian 'bruddah', whose Platinum LP *Facing Future* was released in 1993, Hawaii and the uke started to regain their cool.

Israel Kamakawiwo'ole (1959–97)

THE HAWAIIAN 'BRUDDAH' WHO MADE THE UKE COOL AGAIN

Probably more than any other Hawaiian, Israel Kamakawiwo'ole made the ukulele cool *and* united the people of Hawaii. He was popularly known as 'Iz', and it is an indication of his status as an icon that this abbreviation is now a registered trademark (which means we have to write it as IZ®). His album *Facing Future* from 1993, with its famous medley of 'Somewhere Over the Rainbow' and 'Wonderful World', featuring Hawaiian chant, has sold over two million copies, and its songs have been licensed for use in countless movies and ads.

Brought up in a suburb of Hawaii's capital city, Honolulu, Kamakawiwo'ole (pronounced *kamaka-vee-vo-oh-lay*) was the son of a truck driver (Henry) and a housewife (Evangeline). From early childhood he both overate and made trouble. When taunted about his weight, he would fight back, and was thrown off the school bus virtually every day. During the summer holidays he lived in the countryside, where he was exposed to traditional Hawaiian culture. This was at a time when many Hawaiians, including Israel, could not speak Hawaiian, and instead spoke pidgin English.

Israel began playing the uke at the age of six, and his greatest influence while growing up was the guitar legend Gabby Pahinui. By eleven the talented boy had jobs singing on boats, and in 1971, when his uncle Moe joined Eddie Kamae's Sons of Hawaii, the hugely influential band that was bringing back the old Hawaiian tunes, Israel would often be invited to jam with the band on stage. In 1973, after his family moved to the rural area of Makaha, Israel became *kolohe*, a troublemaker, in high school. By 1974 he was spending his days on the beach, swimming and playing the uke, rather than in school. He formed a band with his brother Skippy and other truanters. They called themselves Makaha Sons of Ni'ihau, became popular very quickly, and in 1976 they recorded their first album, *No Kristo*.

IZ® with his ukulele (above), giving the Hawaiian *shaka* gesture of greeting. In his day, he was the most popular and influential singer in Hawaii.

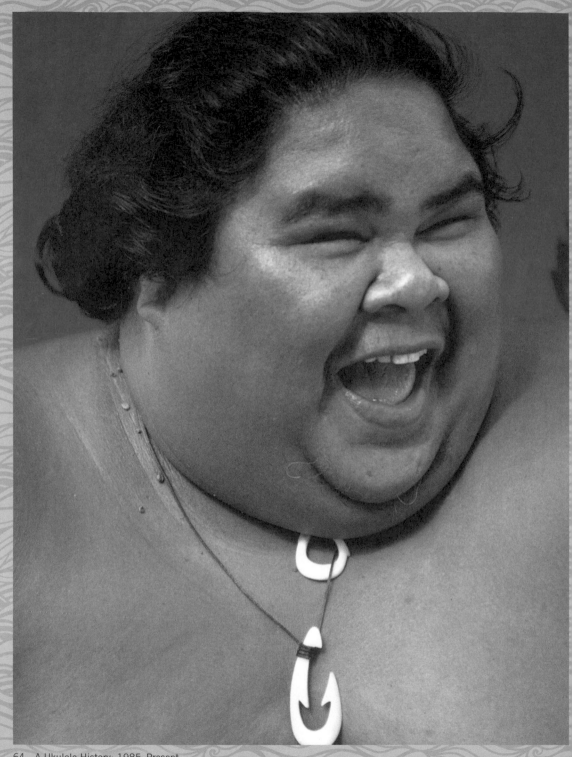

Israel was a tricky character. As well as his addiction to food, he binged on booze, marijuana, cocaine and crystal meth. His hard partying led to chaotic habits: he frequently pulled no-shows at gigs, infuriating fellow band members. But his fondness for a good time also also led him to be seen as a real Hawaiian 'bruddah', one of the people.

The Makaha Sons went on to become one of Hawaii's biggest bands. They travelled all over the islands in their Chevy van, and all started to learn Hawaiian. 'We used to say that we'd sing songs and learn the language later,' said band member Moon. To sing in Hawaiian was a statement of pride in their country, and the Makaha Sons had a political edge.

In 1978 Hawaiian songwriter Mickey Ioane of the D Blahahs of Keaukaha wrote a gentle protest song called 'Hawai'i 78'. It was inspired by a protest of that year, when 51 Hawaiians had clashed with the Army National Guard, and bemoans the effect of the modern world and the American annexation of the late 19th century on the islands of Hawaii. The song asks how King Kalakaua and Queen Lili'uokalani would feel if they came back and saw the highways, railroad tracks, traffic lights and condominiums that have been built over their sacred grounds. A version of the song appears on *Facing Future*, and to date has been viewed over three million times on YouTube.

For most of his career, Israel left the business side to others, and he suffered financially. Music writer Dan Kois says that in 1991, despite all his success, Israel was on welfare and deeply in debt. During one of his frequent hospital stays, he took the advice of lawyer John Ferrigno and joined Jon de Mello's Mountain Apple record label. He also changed

(Above) Israel Kamakawiwo'ole, shown on the right, formed Makaha Sons of Ni'ihau with his brother Skippy, Jerome Koko, Louis Kauakahi and Sam Gray. They released their first album, *No Kristo*, in 1976.

(Opposite) IZ® summed up the allure of the uke when he said: 'What I do is minimum effort, but maximum pleasure. That's part of being Hawaiian, brah.'

FACING   FUTURE

IZ
ISRAEL
KAMAKAWIWO'OLE

IZ®'s 1993 album *Facing Future*, on the
Mountain Apple label, has sold over
two million copies.

his stage name to IZ® as a branding initiative. The move was resented by some islanders: it seemed to them that he was leaving the 'bruddahs' and joining the sharp businessmen.

The two men got IZ® working hard to record *Facing Future*. Miraculously, he turned up on time and stayed the course in the studio. The album mixes old-style Hawaiian songs with *hapa haole* (half white) songs. For example, IZ®'s version of 'Take Me Home Country Roads' is played in a style called Jawaiian, a fusion of reggae and Hawaiian music.

Given his mighty weight, just moving IZ® around to gigs was a huge effort. A whole posse of helpers was required, as well as oxygen canisters. Later in his career IZ® became a born-again Christian and renounced drugs: 'I make a call to all my bruddahs out there, smoking the *batu* [crystal meth], dealing the coke,' he announced in a 1996 television broadcast. 'Stop all the Koreans from bringing in the stuff. Stop the demand, stop the supply ... Hawaiians gonna live on ... when you put Jesus in your heart, you born again. All the *opala* [trash] gone.'

In June 1997, at the age of 38, IZ® died of respiratory problems caused by his obesity. The nation mourned and flags all over Hawaii were flown at half mast. Nearly 50 family members made a giant coffin out of koa wood and thousands of people attended the official funeral. The following weekend thousands more turned out when IZ®'s ashes were thrown into the sea. Lorry drivers parked and sounded their horns. Musician Roland Cazimero, who played bass on *Facing Future*, said: 'From out there it sounded like an island was crying.'

Other pioneers in the Nineties included Kelly Boy Delima of Kapena and Troy Fernandez of the Ka'au Crater Boys. Roy Sakuma, founder of Hawaii's annual ukulele festival in 1971, also opened a ukulele studio. He says that until IZ® and the others appeared, the kids just wanted to learn Western pop songs: 'IZ®, Kapena [and] Ka'au Crater Boys changed all that. Troy came out playing the ukulele like no one had ever heard before. Suddenly all these kids were coming in to learn what Troy was doing on the ukulele.' Troy brought jazz and reggae influences to the instrument. Today he teaches and is widely respected by the younger Hawaiians.

In the US it was Jim Beloff of Connecticut, a great ukulele fan, who really pushed the Third Wave. Jim was a guitarist and worked as associate publisher of *Billboard* magazine. He converted to the uke in 1992, having picked up a lovely old

Jim Beloff is a key figure in the uke's Third Wave. He helped market the Fluke (Tiki King model, right), Flea and Firefly ukuleles that are manufactured by his brother-in-law.

Ukes on the Net

Each wave of ukulele popularity has been pushed forward by a new communication technology: the first by radio, the second by TV, and the third by the Internet, which allows uke fans to share and connect with each other globally. With the Net, you can find the uke chords to most songs in a matter of seconds. When struggling over a sheet of lyrics and chords, the original music, whether a Hawaiian song, a Tin Pan Alley classic or a contemporary tune, is just a mouse click away. You can also listen to the original version on YouTube. Generous teachers, such as Ukulele Mike (right) and the Dominator, put their video tutorials on the web for free. And websites like Ukulele Underground and Ukulele Hunt (see Resources, page 138) bring all these elements together.

YouTube's one-and-only Ukulele Mike.

John King (1953–2009)

KING OF CLASSICAL UKULELE

The *Journal for the Society of American Music* called John King 'perhaps the only truly classical ukulele virtuoso'. However, he played the old Hawaiian songs beautifully as well, having spent some years in Hawaii as a child, and remained in love with the place, amassing a collection of 400 Hawaiian shirts. He took up the guitar at the age of eleven, but decided to explore the ukulele when he discovered that, like certain small guitars of the Renaissance, it used re-entrant tuning. He played in the baroque style, where each note is allowed to sing out like a bell, but commented: 'The truth is it's a crazy way to play the uke; ease of execution is all but sacrificed, subordinated to whatever it takes to get that shimmering, harplike sound. It works for me because when I play it that way, the ukulele sings.' King taught guitar at Eckerd College in Tampa Bay, Florida, until his early death at the age of 55. At the time of his demise he was working on *The 'Ukulele: A History* with Jim Tranquada, and was considered the world authority on the history of the instrument. His beautiful renditions of Bach's Prelude, 'Aloha Oe' and many more can be found on YouTube, where you can also find him playing a replica of an 1850 *machete*.

The late John King performing in 2007. His genius was to demonstrate that the ukulele is ideally suited to playing baroque music.

Ukulele Clubs and Societies

From the Taunton Strummers in the west of England to the Colorado River Uke Group in the USA, and from the Melbourne Ukulele Kollective in Australia to the Ukulele Boudoir of Paris, France, the world is full of ukulele clubs and societies. Everywhere, it seems, people are making music and creating their own entertainment. All you need is a room, some booze and a few cheery uke players. And if you're new in town or just want to extend your social circle, a ukulele club is a great way to meet people: turn up with your uke and you'll find a welcoming crowd. Boundaries tumble down thanks to the power of this mighty little guitar.

A uke group in London's Idler Academy.

Martin tenor instrument in a flea market. He started to publish uke books in 1993, and in *The Ukulele: A Visual History*, which came out in 1997, he cites *The Beatles Anthology* film of 1995 as a key factor in the re-emergence of the ukulele. Paul McCartney says that when he meets 'grown-ups who play the uke, I love 'em.' In 1998 Jim and his wife quit their jobs and started their own ukulele company, Flea Market Music Inc. The following year they introduced a new ukulele to the market. The Fluke, designed by Jim's brother-in-law, has racked up sales of over 50,000, and more than half a million of their *Jumpin' Jim's* songbooks are in print. Truly, the Beloffs found freedom through the uke. Said Jim in a recent interview: 'The ukulele has allowed us to make a living doing what we love, so I guess it means everything.'

Elsewhere in the Nineties the uke thrived, notably in Canada, where the great contemporary player James Hill was a schoolboy beneficiary of J. Chalmers Doane's vision. The uke as a teaching aid for kids has also taken off in Britain, where primary schools are ditching the morose recorder in favour of the friendly uke.

In Japan the story is also positive. The Japanese uke store Kiwaya displays the slogan: 'Offering

Japan's love affair with Hawaiian music lives on with the Sweet Hollywaiians.

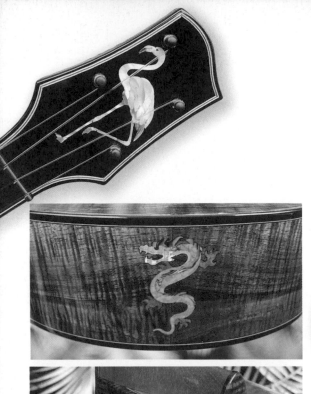

The custom ukes by Chuck Moore of Moore Bettah Ukuleles all boast intricate shell inlays – from the standard tenor uke (right) to the outlandish double-necked ukulele (above right). Based on the Big Island of Hawaii, where his workshop is powered entirely by solar energy, Chuck won Best of Show at the 2012 Big Island Ukulele Guild Show.

Happiness through the Ukulele'. Founded in 1919 as a gramophone repair company, the shop has settled down into a uke school, retailer and manufacturer. Today young groups, such as the Sweet Hollywaiians, wave the flag for Japan's enduring love affair with Hawaii.

In London the uke boom really took off around 2005. That was the year when Matthew Reynolds opened his visionary East London shop, the Duke of Uke, which sells ukes and banjos and puts on courses and events. The shop continues to thrive and, partly thanks to Matthew's influence, there are ukulele clubs all over the country.

Ukuleles bring freedom, to be sure, but they can also bring peace. This is the belief of Israel resident and musician Paul Moore, who uses the power of the ukulele to unite Jew and Arab in the Holy Land. His slogan is: 'From conflict to coexistence: creating opportunities for Jewish and Arab children to meet and become involved with one another in their daily lives.' Paul, a UK-born former stockbroker, says: 'I would love to turn up

Jake Shimabukuro (1976-)

VIRTUOSO HAWAIIAN UKE PLAYER

One of today's biggest young ukulele stars, the Hawaiian Jake Shimabukuro is a fifth-generation Japanese-American, who took up the ukulele at the age of four. He was originally taught traditional Hawaiian music by his mother, but then studied for seven years with Tami Akiyami at Honolulu's Roy Sakuma Studios. He also played the drums with the Kaimuki High School marching band, and says that drumming improved his uke technique. Following a few years playing with a band called Pure Heart, he went solo in 2001 and was signed by the Epic label. His virtuosic 2006 cover version of George Harrison's 'While My Guitar Gently Weeps' on YouTube shot him to fame, and has received over ten million views. His ambitious album *Grand Ukulele* features more cover versions, with backing from an orchestra, although his choice of songs by Sting and Adele perhaps shows a lapse of taste. Respect to him though: he has been called the 'Jimi Hendrix of the ukulele' by *Guitar Player* magazine, has played all over the world and stunned audiences with his technical mastery. Eddie Vedder of Pearl Jam has said of Shimabukuro: 'Jake is taking the instrument to a place that I can't see anybody else catching up with.'

Jake Shimabukuro: 'The Jimi Hendrix of the ukulele.'

Ukuleles for Peace is a project run by Israel resident Paul Moore (above). His aim is to bring Jewish and Arab children together through the power of the ukulele.

at the United Nations and simply play our music to them as a statement of what is possible. Words seem only to divide, whereas music unites us all in harmony.'

The uke has been taken up by various pop stars, including Stephen Merritt of Magnetic Fields. Most notable, though, is Pearl Jam's Eddie Vedder, who has released an album of uke tunes. 'Music just started coming out of this thing,' he said. 'Somehow melodies happen on the uke that I just wasn't pulling out of the guitar.' More improbably, billionaire investor Warren Buffett is also a uke player. You can see him singing 'Ain't She Sweet' on YouTube.

There are loads of great young uke artists out there today. Singer/songwriter Sophie Madeleine of the UK stands out, and a quick list of other great groups and individuals might include Bosko and Honey, Matt Dahlberg, Ralph Shaw, Victoria Vox,

The Ukulele Orchestra of Great Britain

THE UK'S 'DEPRAVED' MUSICOLOGISTS

Formed in 1985, the Ukulele Orchestra of Great Britain was a great success from the outset. Their first gig at a London pub was packed. Founder and musical director George Hinchliffe says: 'We'd put an advert in [listings mag] *City Limits*. People came, people liked it, we did another gig. We got a Radio 1 session and then a BBC live TV thing, and [poet/comedian] John Hegley invited us to play at his club night. We made an album, then we got a phone call from CBS.'

The idea behind the orchestra was not to form a comedy act, though they are undeniably funny, but to create a liberating musical forum where any music could be played, from funk to rock'n'roll to classical. And the ukulele was the right instrument to do that. It was chosen for its musical versatility rather than its novelty value.

Says Hinchliffe: 'The humour only came in during the first gig, when we played in two keys by accident, and were messing around with the sheet music falling everywhere. I thought we should go with it.' They put on dinner jackets and played their gigs seated, in an affectionate parody of a real orchestra. Highlights have included playing to 170,000 people in Hyde Park at the 50-year commemoration of VE Day. They have also played to huge crowds at festivals such as Glastonbury, Womad and the Big Chill.

The 'Ukes', as they are known, play a huge variety of cover versions, from 'Shaft' and 'Anarchy in the UK' to 'Life on Mars' and 'Wuthering Heights'. Their versions somehow shine a new light on the original: you hear the lyrics more clearly and get a better understanding of the mechanics of the song. This is a band of music lovers, and the Ukes call their own style 'depraved musicology'.

The Ukulele Orchestra of Great Britain do the uke salute at the Queen's Hall, Edinburgh, in 2012.

James Hill (1980–)

SINGER, SONGWRITER, AND THE FUTURE OF THE UKULELE

Cheerful Canadian James Hill stands out from many of today's ukulele stars in that as well as playing superb vaudevillian cover versions on the uke, notably 'Billie Jean', he is also an accomplished country-folk songwriter. He was brought up in Langley, British Columbia, where ukulele instruction was on the school curriculum, thanks to pioneering music teacher J. Chalmers Doane. He has released four albums, including the award-winning *True Love Don't Weep*, which demonstrate his joy, passion, virtuosity and humour. He is a dedicated uke evangelist and combines his recording and performing career with teaching. Co-author with Doane of *Ukulele in the Classroom*, a series of method books for teachers, the tireless Hill also edits *Ukulele Yes!* – the quarterly e-zine for uke instructors, runs the educational James Hill Ukulele Initiative, and is director of the annual Langley Ukulele Workshop. Uke expert Jim Beloff has said of Hill: '[His] technique is a seamless blend of speed, accuracy and expressiveness ... a glimpse into the future of the ukulele.'

Canadian musician and teacher James Hill has been called the 'future of the ukulele' by Jim Beloff.

the Singapore Ukulele Movement, Craig Brandau, Uni and Her Ukulele, and Rose Turtle Ertler. Avant-garde duo Buke and Gase feature a six-string baritone ukulele, and actress Zooey Deschanel plays the uke too. Apologies for any we've missed: the scene is changing every day.

You can catch the Third Wave uke players at one of the many festivals around the world. Besides the Ukulele Festival of Hawaii, which has been running since 1971, there are the Cairns Ukulele Festival and the Blue Mountains Ukulele Festival in Australia, the Ukulele Festival of Great Britain in Cheltenham, the Wukulele Festival in Worthing on Britain's south coast, and the Ukulele Festival of Northern California, founded in 1994.

There's no doubt about it – the uke is liberating and a force for good, and there has never been a better time to learn it than today. This cheerful small guitar is truly the instrument of the people. With one in your hand, you turn from consumer to producer. Free your spirit, play the uke!

Sophie Madeleine (above) is a British singer/songwriter and uke player. Her 2009 album was called *Love. Life. Ukulele.*

A Soprano GB Custom ukulele (right), with Adirondack spruce top and curly koa back and sides, made by the DaSilva Ukulele Company of Berkeley, California. DaSilva are considered by many to be among the best ukulele makers in the world today.

How to Play
the Ukulele

Before You Begin

If you don't already own a ukulele, here is some advice about buying one, as well as information for left-handed players, and suggestions for how to structure your progress through our six-week course for learning to play the instrument.

I. Buying a Ukulele

CHOOSING THE RIGHT SIZE

Ukuleles come in a range of sizes. These are known, smallest first, as soprano, concert, tenor and baritone (see below). The beginner is not advised to choose a baritone uke. It has a similar sound to a guitar and unlike the others, is usually tuned to DGBE, like the top four strings of a guitar. In other words, you might as well just get a guitar, unless you are a ukulele purist. The choice for most uke players is between a soprano, concert and tenor size.

For your first ukulele, we recommend you choose a soprano. This is considered the standard size as it has the dimensions of the original early Hawaiian instruments. Sopranos can be slightly cheaper than the larger sizes, but more important for a beginner is that it has a small neck with close-together strings. This means that it is a little easier to stretch for the more difficult chords. Sopranos also tend to have a brighter, punchier tone.

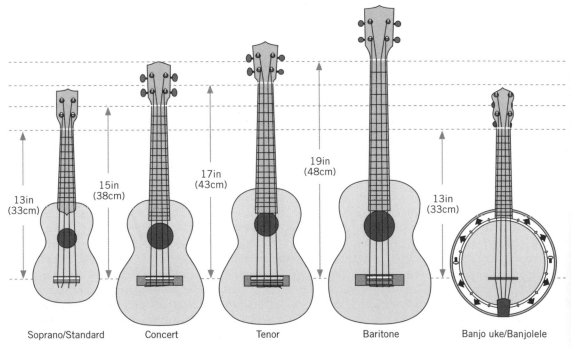

| 13in (33cm) | 15in (38cm) | 17in (43cm) | 19in (48cm) | 13in (33cm) |

| Soprano/Standard | Concert | Tenor | Baritone | Banjo uke/Banjolele |

Some find, however, that the short, narrow neck of the soprano feels cramped, especially when their ukulele playing improves and they start playing notes and chords higher up the fretboard. The best thing to do is to try out the sizes in a music shop to see which feels best.

If you already own a soprano and are thinking of getting another ukulele, it is a good idea to add a concert or tenor uke to your collection. The tenor, being the larger of the two, has a warmer tone (approaching that of a guitar). Like the concert type, it is a little louder than the soprano because its soundboard (the wood on the front of the instrument that amplifies the strings' vibrations) has a larger area. But if it is volume you want, you could always try a banjo uke, or 'banjolele'. This has a skin on the front, like a drum, which makes the sound quite different. It is more of a metallic, percussive, banjo-like sound, which is great for the syncopated strumming that George Formby made his own (see page 41).

THE TYPE OF WOOD

One of the main factors determining the cost of a ukulele is what it is made of. The wood in cheaper ukes tends to be laminated, which means an attractive veneer is bonded onto a cheaper wood. Solid wood ukes, in which each panel (or at least the top panel) is made of a single piece of wood, are more expensive. If a ukulele's sales description makes no mention of solid wood, it is most likely laminate. This can be fine for a starter ukulele. In fact, laminate ukes can be more robust – less likely to warp and crack in the harsh temperature and humidity variations caused by central heating. However, a laminate uke has less depth of tone and, unlike solid wood, its sound doesn't improve with age. So if you can stretch to a uke with a solid wood top, do.

Along with the type of strings (see page 114), the thickness and type of wood used for the top of a solid-wood ukulele are the most important factors in determining how it sounds. Koa, a native hardwood of Hawaii, is the traditional option. It is what all the early soprano ukuleles were made

Uke strings are tuned by adjusting the keys at the end of the neck. Friction tuners (top) are more traditional than geared or machine tuners (bottom). It is a safer bet to go for geared when you are starting out, as they tend to hold tune better and don't require fiddling with a screwdriver to adjust their tightness. Geared tuners allow more sensitive adjustments, which make all the difference when tuning.

of, and its warm, rich tone is considered by many to be the perfect choice to enrich the naturally 'plinky' sound of such a small instrument. But its relative scarcity these days means that it is one of the more expensive options. Mahogany is cheaper, far more common, and has a warm tone like koa, so is a great choice for a more affordable soprano. When it comes to the larger concert and tenor sizes, spruce can be a good and affordable option. Its bright, punchy tone means that these larger instruments still keep the distinctive ukulele sound associated with the traditional soprano size. At the end of the day, it is simply a matter of which sound you like best of the ukes in your price range.

BUYING IN A SHOP OR ON THE INTERNET

Since the right sound for you is so subjective, it is better by far to buy from a real shop rather than on the Internet. Not only does this let you compare the sounds and ask advice, it also allows you to check a few essentials before you part with your money. You should favour a uke with a low 'action', which means that the strings, when viewed side on, are as close as possible to the fretboard, without being so close as to buzz when held down at any of the frets. The lower the action, the easier it is to play. Buying on the Internet is no problem if you know what you are looking for, but always check the returns policy in case it's not what you expect.

BRANDS TO CONSIDER FOR ENTRY-LEVEL UKES

You can spend hundreds on a uke, but a perfectly good one can be yours for £30–£80. Good entry-level ukes are made by Lanikai, Kala, Ohana, Cordoba and Oscar Schmidt, but if cheapness is paramount, you can't go wrong with a Makala 'Dolphin', which has a wooden top with plastic back and sides. Just remember, cheaper ukes tend to come with cheap strings. Quality ones don't cost much and will make a huge difference to the sound, so see page 114 for information about buying new strings and re-stringing your ukulele.

Buying Vintage

If you are prepared to do some careful research and ask probing questions of the seller, you can find beautiful vintage ukuleles from the Thirties on eBay for a few hundred pounds. However, many old ukes have cracks, and you need to work out whether they are cosmetic or structural. If a crack is structural, the instrument will need to be looked at by a trained luthier before it is any use. If you are lucky, you might be able to find an original made in Hawaii of traditional koa wood. The Tabu stamp (left) was a trademarked symbol that Hawaiian ukulele manufacturers often burnt onto their ukuleles to prove that they were genuinely made on the islands. Appearing on ukes from 1915 to the early Thirties, it was a response to unscrupulous makers on the US mainland who were passing off their instruments as Hawaiian made. The word *tabu* is ancient Polynesian for 'forbidden', and passed into English as 'taboo'. The symbol incorporates two crossed *kapu* staffs – weapons that were used to enforce the rule of law in old Hawaii, and they served as a clear message to the mainland imitators. To this day, the Tabu stamp assures anyone looking to buy a ukulele from this period that an instrument is a genuine Hawaiian-made original.

2. Left-handed players

If you are left-handed, you can use the same instrument as a right-handed player, but you will need to string your ukulele the other way around. Each of the strings has a different thickness that is appropriate for the note it is intended to be tuned to. For example, the 3rd string, tuned to a C, needs to be one designed for that tuning. If you buy your first uke from a music shop, you could ask if they will re-string it for a left-handed player. You might also need to change the nut (shown below) to avoid buzzing strings, since the grooves for a right-handed tuning will no longer match the string thicknesses. Measure the dimensions of your nut and order a matching left-handed one online. Prise out the old nut and slip in the new. See page 114 for information and advice on re-stringing a ukulele yourself. The diagram below shows the correct order for the strings. Use this diagram for the tuning instructions in the first week of this uke course rather than the one on page 82. (The photographs throughout the How to Play section show right-handed tunings.)

Your head is up here as you play it

See page 82 about tuning

4th string –> tune to g
(This is always the string nearest your head as you play.)

3rd string –> tune to C

2nd string' –> tune to E

1st string –> tune to A
(This is always the string nearest your feet as you play.)

You might need to change the nut

The order in which the strings should go for a left handed player is the opposite of that for a right-handed player.

3. Planning your six weeks

We've divided our How to Play the Ukulele course into six weeks, but there is no obligation for you to stick to this schedule. Of course, you can take as long or as short a time for each week as feels right. Whatever pace you go at, remember that you'll pick up the chords and techniques best if you progress at a steady pace, digesting the new material and then coming back to it next time to consolidate and practise what you have learned before moving on. The best practice routine is always a little and often. It is amazing how your subconscious mind gets to work on new techniques while you are getting on with life. Over time, you'll find that each time you return to practise a tricky chord or strumming technique, it seems a little easier than it did when you last finished practising.

Week One

First things first – let's get your uke tuned up. After that we'll cover the basics of holding it, strumming it and positioning your fingers to produce a clear note. This week, you'll learn to read chord diagrams to master two simple uke chords. We'll strum these in a basic way to accompany your first song. It may sound good, it may sound rubbish, but you've got to start somewhere and that somewhere is here …

1. Tuning to g, C, E, A

While buying a uke doesn't have to be expensive, the downside of getting a cheap instrument is that it can go out of tune easily. Confidence in tuning is therefore essential. A uke even slightly out of tune will sound terrible no matter how well you play it.

There is more than one set of notes that the strings of a ukulele can be tuned to. Throughout this book, we are going to stick to the g, C, E, A tuning because it is what most people use and means the chords are easy for C, the most common key.

You have to pluck an open string and twiddle the tuning key to change the pitch up or down until it is sounding the correct note. Here are three ways to get the correct notes.

USE AN ELECTRONIC TUNER OR APP One or other is by far the best solution (see below), since you have to tune a uke often. A tuning app for your smartphone is the slightly cheaper option.
TUNE IT TO ANOTHER INSTRUMENT Obviously, the other instrument has to be in tune! A piano or electronic keyboard is a good bet (see right).
TUNE IT TO ITSELF This ensures the strings are at least in tune with each other. This method is more complicated and not as useful as those above, so we'll look at it in Week Four.

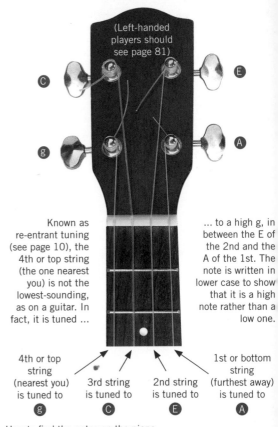

(Left-handed players should see page 81)

Known as re-entrant tuning (see page 10), the 4th or top string (the one nearest you) is not the lowest-sounding, as on a guitar. In fact, it is tuned …

… to a high g, in between the E of the 2nd and the A of the 1st. The note is written in lower case to show that it is a high note rather than a low one.

4th or top string (nearest you) is tuned to **g**

3rd string is tuned to **C**

2nd string is tuned to **E**

1st or bottom string (furthest away) is tuned to **A**

How to find the notes on the piano:

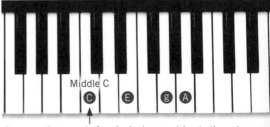

Middle C

Compare the sound of a plucked open string to the notes on a keyboard. Ask a grown-up to show you which is middle C.

A clip-on electronic tuner (left) or a smartphone app shows the note you are playing on a display. As you twiddle the key, you'll see when you are getting close to the desired note.

2. Holding your uke

Let's not get too fancy about how to hold your ukulele. The main thing is to make sure your strumming hand is free to move up and down at the wrist while your forearm holds the uke against your body. It is easier when you are sitting down, as the bottom of the uke can rest gently on your thigh. Don't grip the uke between your arm and tummy too tightly – it will hinder your strumming movements and dampen the sound.

When it comes to your other hand (your left hand if you are right-handed), the thumb should be behind the neck so that you can press down on the strings with your fingers. By gripping the main body with your strumming arm, you shouldn't need to do much supporting with your other hand. Apart from steadying the uke a bit, that hand should be free to move around the fretboard like a dancing flea.

Up ...

down ...

3. Chord diagrams and playing a C chord

Here is a chord diagram for the chord of C, as well as a photograph to show what it means:

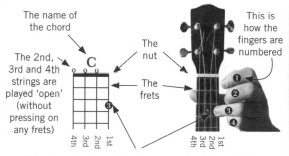

The name of the chord

The 2nd, 3rd and 4th strings are played 'open' (without pressing on any frets)

The nut

The frets

This is how the fingers are numbered

This shows that you should press on the 1st, or bottom, string behind the 3rd fret. The number 3 advises you to use your third (or ring) finger to make the note.

and shake it all around.

This chord of C is very common on the ukulele, so it is a good one to start with. Try making the chord with your third (or ring) finger and then strumming down across all the strings with the pad of your thumb to hear how the chord sounds. You should press firmly on the string with the very end of your third finger, just behind the 3rd fret (which means between the 2nd and 3rd frets). The idea is to hold the string cleanly against the metal of the fret so that the fret acts as the fixed point from which the string vibrates. Check the sound of the 1st string that you are pressing down on by playing this on its own. If you are fretting it right, it should make a clean note that is not buzzy.

There's no denying, the G7 chord is more of a challenge than the C.

4. Your second chord: G7

You need only two chords to play your first songs. The second chord required is called G7. Don't worry too much at this stage how the chord-naming convention works, but the number 7 means that one of the notes that makes up a normal G chord has been changed to make it sound a bit more jazzy.

On the left you'll see the chord diagram and the finger position photograph. G7 is trickier than the C chord because it uses three fingers at the same time, which means you have to be extra careful about each of the strings making a clean note. Before we worry about that, just try positioning your fingers in the right places to match the G7 diagram and photograph. Remember, you want to be pressing down on the strings with the *ends* of your fingers.

5. Keep it clean

Now let's concentrate on the difficult bit: getting each of the four strings to make a clean note. Try playing each string in turn as you hold the G7 chord. If any of them sounds buzzy or deadened, you will need to subtly change your finger positions.

BUZZY NOTES These are usually caused by not holding your finger down firmly enough, or because it is not quite in the right position relative to the fret. You need to hold it just behind the fret, which means your finger should be right next to the fret, but on the side *away from* the sound hole.

DEADENED NOTES This is a common problem with chords that require three or four fingers. There's not much room for your fingers to squeeze next to each other without touching (and so deadening) the neighbouring strings. Make sure you are pressing down on each string with the fingertips. Ukulele and guitar players always have short nails on the fingering hand so that they don't get in the way of pressing down. Try adjusting the position of your fingers slightly until none are touching the neighbouring strings.

CORRECTING BUZZY NOTES: Make sure that you are holding down the string just behind the fret.

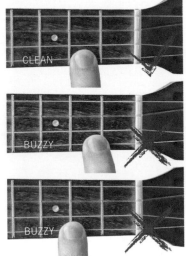

CORRECTING DEADENED NOTES: When playing a G7 chord, the 2nd string is the one that tends to sound deadened because your second finger gets in the way. Make sure you are pressing it down on the tip, and that the 2nd string is unobstructed.

6. The tricky bit is changing chords

The C and the G7 chords are the only ones you need in Week One. In order to use them for a song, you need to become adept at changing from one to the other. This is what you should practise as much as possible because your song will only sound good when you can move your fingers from one chord to the next without breaking the rhythm.

To change from C to G7, remember this important trick: you don't need to lift your third finger off the string as you make the change. Instead, just release the pressure on the string but leave the finger touching it. Now slide the finger along to the 2nd fret (see right) as you bring your first and second fingers into place and press them all down on the fretboard to form the G7 chord.

You can do the same as you change back to the C: releasing the pressure as you slide your third finger back up a fret and removing your first and second fingers. In this way, your third finger acts as a guide for positioning your other two fingers. As you slide it along the string, you can feel it pass over the fret, which means that you know when it is in the right position without having to look. In time, you won't need to look in order to add the other two fingers to make the G7. Being able to change chords without looking is a very useful skill because it means you can keep your eyes on the song sheet and play the ukulele during a power cut.

7. Your first song

C and G7 are all you need to sing the nursery rhyme 'London Bridge' (see overleaf). Let's keep things as simple as possible when it comes to your strumming hand. Just sound the chord by using the pad of your thumb to strum downwards across all the strings. Strum once on each beat. The beats are shown on the music as either a chord diagram or a slash symbol, and both mean the same thing: strum the chord. Hold your fingers down on the fretboard in between strums so that the notes of the chords continue to ring out.

Your main aim with this song should be to try to make the change between the C and G7 chords as fluid as possible. You want to go from one to the other without slowing the rhythm of the strums. It is far better to slow the song right down so that you can make the chord transitions in between the beats than it is to play it at normal speed and have to break the rhythm at the chord changes. As you get better at sliding your third finger along a fret while adding or removing the first and second fingers, you will find that you can gradually increase the speed. For the time being, start playing 'London Bridge' as if it's a restful and languorous lullaby – you know, for a baby that you hope will grow up to become a structural engineer ...

C

G7

To change from C to G7, don't lift your third finger off the string, but simply lessen the pressure and slide it down a fret.

London Bridge

First note: The note you should start singing with is a G. This is the open 4th or top string:

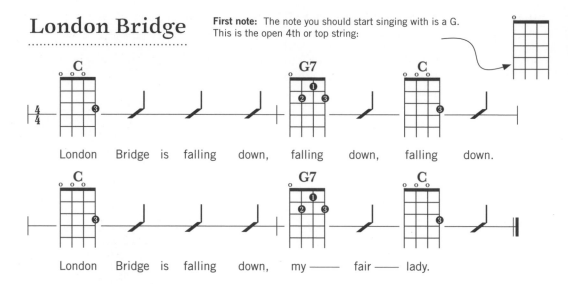

London   Bridge   is   falling   down,   falling   down,   falling   down.

London   Bridge   is   falling   down,   my —— fair —— lady.

(C) Build it up with wood and clay, **(G7)** wood and clay, **(C)** wood and clay. **(C)** Build it up with wood and clay, **(G7)** my fair **(C)** lady.

(C) Wood and clay will wash away, **(G7)** wash away, **(C)** wash away. **(C)** Wood and clay will wash away, **(G7)** my fair **(C)** lady.

Build it up with bricks and mortar, ... / ... my fair lady.
    Bricks and mortar will not stay, ... / ... my fair lady.
Build it up with iron and steel, ... / ... my fair lady.
    Iron and steel will bend and bow, ... / ... my fair lady.
Build it up with silver and gold, ... / ... my fair lady.
    Silver and gold will be stolen away, ... / ... my fair lady.
Set a man to watch all night, ... / ... my fair lady.
    Suppose the man should fall asleep, ... / ... my fair lady.
Give him a pipe to smoke all night, ... / ... my fair lady.

(Repeat until you couldn't care less about London Bridge, but can go from C –> G7 –> C without slowing your rhythm.)

8. Practising

A metronome (or a metronome smartphone app) slowed right down can help you keep time as you practise the chord changes of a new song.

As with anything new, the best way to learn the ukulele is by practising little and often. Ten minutes three times a day is better than half an hour in one go. Your subconscious mind will rehearse the muscle signals for making the chords as you get on with life. (It will also probably change the words into something about your mother.) You will find that it is a little easier to play the chords each time you return. As always, concentrate on changing between the C and G7 chords without breaking the rhythm. It can be helpful to use a metronome (or a metronome app on your smartphone) to slow everything right down. When you are bored with bridges, try to work out two other songs that use C and G7: 'Oh My Darling, Clementine' and 'He's Got the Whole World in His Hands'.

Week Two

We will introduce a third chord that will enormously expand the potential of your uke repertoire, but we will be mainly concentrating on your strumming hand. This week is all about introducing rhythm to your uke playing and noticing how the fingers you strum with change the sound.

1. The tone of your strum

The positioning of your fingers on the fretboard determines the notes and chords on your ukulele, but the way you strum the strings with your other hand determines the all-important rhythm.

Before we look at the timing of your strums, let's get the sound right. You'll want to find your ukulele's 'sweet spot'. This is the strumming position that makes the richest and fullest sound. Holding down the C chord that we learned last week, strum down over all the strings with your thumb. Notice how the tone of the chord sounds warmer or tinnier depending on whether you strum near the 'saddle' (see right), the sound hole or where the neck meets the body. You should strum in the position that sounds best to you, but you'll usually get the richest sound by strumming around where the neck meets the body.

Your strum will also sound very different depending on which part of which finger you use. Fancy multi-finger rolls aside, there are three basic options: strumming with your thumb, your forefinger or a combination of the two. Try a single downward strum over all the strings to hear how the sound differs with each.

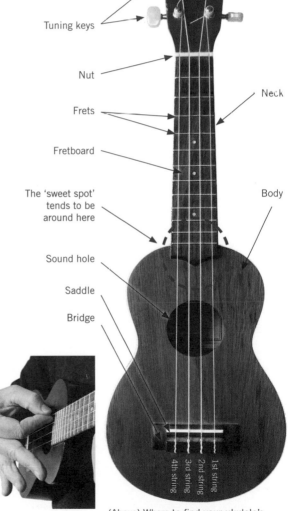

Head (or headstock)

Tuning keys

Nut

Neck

Frets

Fretboard

The 'sweet spot' tends to be around here

Body

Sound hole

Saddle

Bridge

4th string / 3rd string / 2nd string / 1st string

(Above) Where to find your ukulele's 'sweet spot' – and all the other bits too.

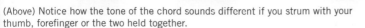

(Above) Notice how the tone of the chord sounds different if you strum with your thumb, forefinger or the two held together.

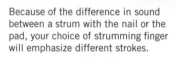

Thumb: The emphasis falls naturally on the upstrokes:

down – UP – down – UP – down – UP – down – UP

Forefinger: Emphasis falls naturally on the downstrokes:

DOWN – up – DOWN – up – DOWN – up – DOWN – up

Thumb & forefinger: Emphasis is naturally the same for both:

DOWN – UP – DOWN – UP – DOWN – UP – DOWN – UP

Because of the difference in sound between a strum with the nail or the pad, your choice of strumming finger will emphasize different strokes.

Should you ever strum a ukulele with a guitar pick?

Nope.

Your fingernail makes a loud, punchy sound, while the fleshy pad of your finger or thumb makes a gentler, warmer sound. Try strumming your hand up and down over the strings at a regular pace. Using your thumb gives an emphasis on the upstrokes, while using your forefinger gives an emphasis on the downstrokes. If you strum with both together, the emphasis depends more on how much force you apply to the strings on any stroke. Experiment with different fingers for different songs. By the way, you should never use a guitar pick to strum a ukulele. On such small strings, they sound terrible. Some people use felt picks, which are designed for use on ukes, but we feel that it is far more sensible to stick to strumming with your fingers. As you get more proficient at the uke, you will want to introduce rolls and other fancy twiddles (see Week Six), which can't be done with a pick.

2. Introducing the third chord: F

You can't play many songs with just two chords. By learning a third – the chord of F – you'll find that a whole world of musical possibilities will open up. Here is how to play an F chord:

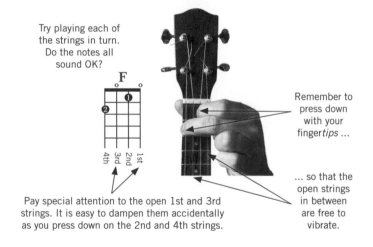

Try playing each of the strings in turn. Do the notes all sound OK?

Remember to press down with your finger*tips* ...

... so that the open strings in between are free to vibrate.

Pay special attention to the open 1st and 3rd strings. It is easy to dampen them accidentally as you press down on the 2nd and 4th strings.

Once you've positioned your fingers correctly so that each of the four strings makes a nice clean note, it is time to practise the all-important skill of changing from one chord to another. The smoothness of these changes makes the difference between a fluent performance and a faltering one.

You do not always need to take your fingers off the fretboard when you change between C, G7 and F. We've already seen that your third finger can just slide one fret along the 1st string as you change between C and G7. When you change between F and G7, your first finger doesn't need to move at all. The chord change is much easier if you just leave that finger in place. Try changing between the three chords as you strum in simple, steady downward strokes with your thumb. Slow the rate of your strums until they are sedate enough for you to make the chord changes without having to break the rhythm. If you have access to a metronome or metronome phone app, set it very slow and strum along. It doesn't matter how slow you set it. The important thing is to get used to changing chords while maintaining the rhythm. When we introduce more syncopated strumming to accompany this week's song, you will want to learn to do it correctly and slowly rather than fast and fumblingly.

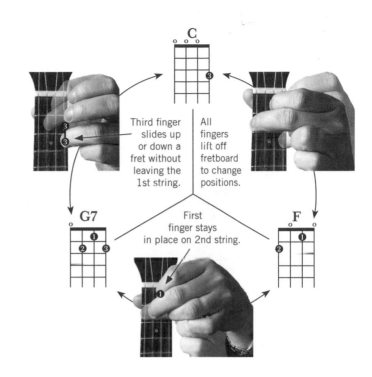

As you practise changing between C, F and G7, notice how some fingers can slide along a string or simply stay in place.

3. Three essential strumming patterns

As well as a repertoire of chords, you should learn a range of different strumming rhythms or patterns. These will let you vary your playing style and find strums to match the song you are singing. Here, for starters, are three basic strums. They are all for pieces in 4/4 time, which means that there are four beats in every bar – the sort of songs that you count in with 1, 2, 3, 4 ...

THE STRAIGHT SHUFFLE This is the most basic, generic strum, and couldn't be simpler. You strum down on each of the four beats in the bar, and up on the 'ands' between. The downstrokes and the upstrokes are all of equal duration. Hold an F chord (right) and strum up and down steadily with your forefinger like this:

Count: **1** – and – **2** – and – **3** – and – **4** – and – ...

Strum: **D** – u – **D** – u – **D** – u – **D** – u – ...

The letters tell you whether it is a downstroke or an upstroke. When the letter is a capital, it means that the stroke has more emphasis.

This 'time signature' tells you that each bar (the basic portion of a musical score) contains four beats, each of which is what's called a quarter note (for more on time signatures, see pages 95–6).

Each beat, or quarter note, can be divided into two equal eighth notes, which are joined with a beam like this.

Strumming is often written down in 'slash notation', which is a sort of musical notation without the notes. Here is how the straight shuffle looks in slash notation, with the counting below:

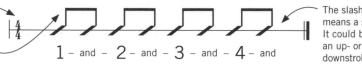

1 – and – 2 – and – 3 – and – 4 – and

The slash means a strum. It could be an up- or a downstroke.

THE JAZZ SHUFFLE This is similar to the straight shuffle, but a little more syncopated. Rather than the down- and upstrokes being of equal duration, the down lasts a little longer than the up. This is like someone walking with a limp rather than the sure and steady pace of the straight shuffle. This time, try it with a C chord, using your forefinger to strum up and down like this:

Dotted notation: When you see a dot after a note (or slash) it means that you extend the note's duration by half as long again. Here the dot after the eighth note means that it lasts for an eighth plus a sixteenth beat. This means that the first of each pair lands on the count, while the second is just before the next count, giving a jazzy, shuffling feel to the rhythm.

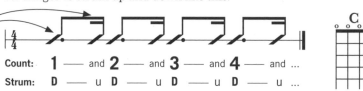

C

Count: 1 —— and 2 —— and 3 —— and 4 —— and ...
Strum: D —— u D —— u D —— u D —— u ...

THE CHURCH LICK Also known as 'bluegrass strumming', the church lick is more complex because two of the 'and' counts in a bar are not strummed. However, you should still count them out as this will help keep everything on track. Forget the limping syncopation of the jazz shuffle; we are back to a steady counting pace. This time, hold a G7 chord and strum with your thumb. After the first downstroke, the thumb comes back up without touching the strings before strumming the down – up – down for counts 2 – and – 3, after which it comes up again without touching the strings, etc. Try emphasizing beats 1 and 3 (as the capital D indicates):

This is a quarter note symbol, which means that the strum lasts for a whole count ('1 and ...'). A quarter note lasts the same duration as two eighth notes.

You count the 'and' but you don't strum it. Instead, you just lift your hand back up without touching the strings (ready for the next downstroke).

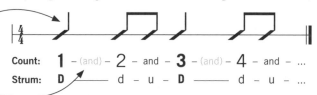

G7

Count: 1 – (and) – 2 – and – 3 – (and) – 4 – and – ...
Strum: D —— d – u – D —— d – u – ...

4. This week's song

Let's try using the church lick to strum along to 'When the Saints Go Marching In'. Remember, you can slow it right down with a metronome so that you have time to do the chord changes without breaking the flow of the song. The strumming slashes are marked in red at the all-important points where the chord changes.

When the Saints Go Marching In

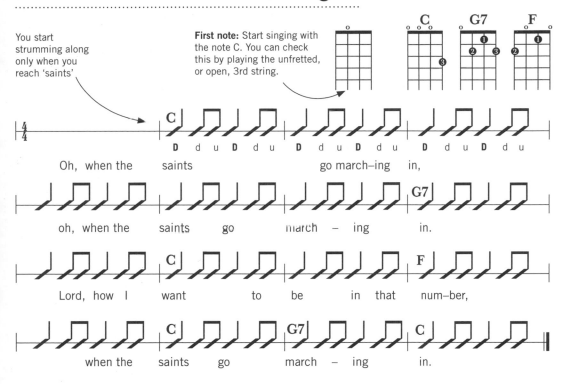

You start strumming along only when you reach 'saints'

First note: Start singing with the note C. You can check this by playing the unfretted, or open, 3rd string.

C   G7   F

$\frac{4}{4}$

C

D   d   u   **D**   d   u   **D**   d   u   **D**   d   u   **D**   d   u   **D**   d   u

Oh, when the   saints   go march–ing   in,

G7

oh, when the   saints   go   march   –   ing   in.

C   F

Lord, how I   want   to   be   in   that   num–ber,

C   G7   C

when the   saints   go   march   –   ing   in.

5. Practising

The best way to build up confidence and versatility in your uke playing is to experiment. As well as using the church lick, try versions of 'When the Saints ...' using the straight shuffle and the jazz shuffle strumming patterns. Listen how changing your strumming pattern can give a different feel to the song. Why not try singing it *really* slowly with nothing more than a gentle downstroke of your thumb on each beat – a slow and simple downward caress of the strings on the counts of 1, 2, 3 and 4 in each bar. With such a slow and steady backing, you could improvise, adding twiddles and fancy bits to the melody that you are singing. This might sound like rubbish or it might be interesting.

To continue practising your chord changes and educating your ear, see if you can work out the chord changes to some of the many other songs that can be played with C, F and G7 (see right). It is really good training for your ear as well as your uke skills to figure out which of the three chords sounds right in which parts of the songs.

> **Try some of the many other songs that can be played with C, F and G7**
> These generally start with the C chord, but if you check with recordings, they might be in a different key. This means you'll have to sing at a different pitch from the recording to use C, F and G7.

> 'You Are My Sunshine'
> 'I Fought The Law'
> (covered by the Clash)
> 'Twinkle, Twinkle, Little Star'
> 'Hound Dog'
> (covered by Elvis Presley)
> 'Twist and Shout' by the Beatles
> (try starting with a bit of G7 before strumming along with C, F, G7...)
> 'Doo Wah Diddy' by Manfred Mann

Week Three

It is time to start playing individual notes on your ukulele in order to play some instrumental music. To help with this, we will learn to read ukulele tablature, or 'tab'. We will also introduce some minor chords, which produce a melancholy tone, and learn about chord families.

1. Getting to know ukulele tabs

Of course, the ukulele is not just for strumming along to a song – it can also be played as a solo instrument. That requires being able to pick out a melody, and to do so, you'll need to learn to read tablature, or 'tab'. This is a way of writing music for stringed instruments, like the ukulele, that have frets. It is a limited form of musical notation: you can't play music written in ukulele tablature on any other instrument, not even a guitar. But tab is the easiest ukulele music notation to pick up as a beginner. For this reason, it is the one we'll use throughout these lessons when we need to show the notes to play rather than just the chords. Here is how ukulele tablature works:

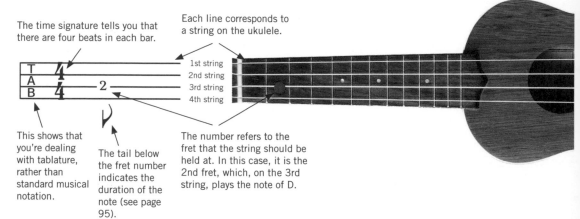

The time signature tells you that there are four beats in each bar.

Each line corresponds to a string on the ukulele.

1st string
2nd string
3rd string
4th string

This shows that you're dealing with tablature, rather than standard musical notation.

The tail below the fret number indicates the duration of the note (see page 95).

The number refers to the fret that the string should be held at. In this case, it is the 2nd fret, which, on the 3rd string, plays the note of D.

Reading tablature can feel a little daunting at first, especially when you've only just got the hang of chord diagrams. One confusion is that the number on the tab refers to the *fret* at which to hold the string, while on chord diagrams, numbers (if there are any) refer to the *fingers* you're advised to use to make the chord.

Another possible confusion is remembering which lines refer to which strings. The top line refers to the 1st string, which is the one furthest away from you as you play the uke, so it's at the bottom! If you get confused while holding the uke, put your strumming hand under the uke body and momentarily turn it so that the front is facing upwards. Now the tab lines and the strings correspond.

(Above) How the lines of ukulele tablature correspond to the strings of the instrument.

Try to play this simple melody by following the tablature below and see if you can tell which heavy rock anthem it is (the red numbers at the top show you how to count the beats):

Of course, it wasn't a rock anthem at all. It was 'Twinkle, Twinkle, Little Star', the drum-and-bass classic.

These tails indicate the duration of the notes (see page 95).

2. Chord families

In order to be strictly accurate about chord names, the C and F chords that you have learned should really be called C major and F major. This is to distinguish them from their minor-chord counterparts. Depending on the context, minor chords can sound a little less jolly than major ones. Of course, it is the differences in the mood of the chords you play that bring emotional colour to a piece.

It is high time, therefore, that you learned a minor chord. One that fits well with the C, F and G7 chords you already know is A minor, and is abbreviated to Am. Thankfully, it is a doddle to play. As you can see to the left, it can be played with open strings and just one finger.

Try playing the Am with the other three chords. Starting with a C chord, just change from one to the other, listening to how they sound together. As you learn to play an instrument, you can become so focused on getting your finger positions and hand movements right that you practically forget to listen to the sound you are creating. Pay attention, therefore, to how the sound of the G7 seems to be calling out for you to return to the resolution of the C with which you started. Remember to slow your strumming right down so that you can do the changes without stopping.

The chords all tend to sound good together, don't they? So long as you began strumming with a C chord, the transitions from one chord to the next tend to work. The reason is because C, F, G7 and Am are all part of the same chord 'family': the C chord family.

All the chords in a chord family are made up of notes taken from the same set or 'scale'. The four chords you know are made of notes found in the scale of C major. Since you now know how to read

(Above) Change between Am and F, leaving your second finger in place and just lifting or placing down your first.

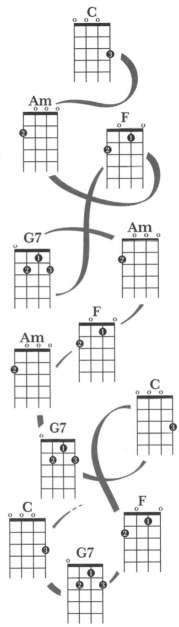

(Above) As you practise changing between the four chords you now know, don't follow a fixed pattern. Go with the flow and listen to how they sound in each other's company.

ukulele tab, it is easy to show you how to play the scale of C major. Remember, the numbers on the tab are nothing to do with the fingers you use. They refer to the fret that the string (represented by the line) is to be held down at to play the note:

The scale of C major, shown in ukulele tablature:

1st ➤
2nd ➤
3rd ➤
4th ➤

Remember which line of the ukulele tablature refers to which string.

When you look at the open strings and the frets you used to make the C, F, G7 and Am chords, you can see that they are all made up of notes from the C major scale. (Of course, they use the notes from the same scale on the 4th or top string too.) The diagrams below show which of the notes from the scale are used for each chord:

When the notes of the C major scale are shown on the fretboard and on a chord diagram, you can see that all the chords in the C chord family are made up of notes from this scale.

These are the positions of the notes in the C major scale ...

... which are used by the chords in the C chord family, like this:

C **G7** **F** **Am**

In fact, there are also a couple more chords that are part of this happy family. They are both minor chords – E minor and D minor – so they would probably feel sorry for themselves if we left them out.

D minor and E minor are the last two members of our C chord family.

Dm **Em**

Since they're members of the C chord family, Dm and Em are, of course, made up of notes drawn from the C major scale too.

Dm **Em**

As you practise playing these last two chords in the family, you should try (as always) moving from one chord to the next to improve the fluidity of your changes. Notice how changing between Am, Dm and F involves minimal finger changes since all three chords share the note A at the 2nd fret of the 4th (or top) string.

So what are you going to do with all these blooming chords? Why not use them to play along to a track such as 'Rhiannon' by Fleetwood Mac? So long as your uke is in tune (see page 82), all the chords should sound pretty good when you play along with a recording. Don't worry about singing. Just pretend you are a ukulele whiz brought in by Fleetwood Mac to add some colour to the accompaniment. When it comes to which chords to use where, just remember always to start off with the Am chord in the verses, and start off with the C chord in the chorus. Other than that, just bumble around with different chords from the C chord family.

Generally, they will fit pretty well. At worst, it will just sound like you are jazzing things up a little. Die-hard Fleetwood Mac fans might wince, but we're sure Stevie Nicks won't mind. Remember, you don't have to do lots of chord changes. Just try strumming a few chords here and there to hear which fit where. For all the goldfish uke players, the C family chord diagrams are shown here, once again. Take it away!

It's time you put your chord family to good use by jamming along to 'Rhiannon' by Fleetwood Mac (below).

Jamming with Fleetwood Mac's 'Rhiannon' and the C family of chords:

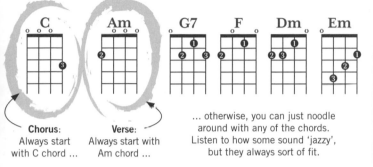

Chorus:
Always start with C chord ...

Verse:
Always start with Am chord ...

... otherwise, you can just noodle around with any of the chords. Listen to how some sound 'jazzy', but they always sort of fit.

3. Getting to know tabs better

Working out notes on ukulele tablature is simple if you remember which lines refer to which strings and that the numbers mean the frets. But what about the rhythm? Often tablature is written beneath standard musical notation (as we've done on pages 122 and 126). In this case, the note durations are clear from the standard notation, so the tabs do not say anything about note duration. When tab is on its own, stems are added below the lines to indicate how long a note lasts. Here's how the stems indicate a whole note (four beats), half note (two beats), quarter note (one beat), eighth note (half a beat) and sixteenth note (quarter of a beat). Standard notation is shown underneath.

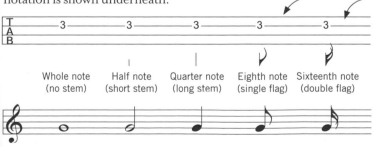

When more than one of these notes are next to each other, they are usually joined with one or more beats (see overleaf).

It seems a little confusing at first that a single beat is described as a quarter note (also called a 'crotchet'), while a whole note (or 'semibreve') lasts four beats. It's just the convention of music notation.

You can see how the different durations compare when you look at the bars of tablature overleaf. The two 4s at the beginning of the tabs are known as the time signature. They tell you how many beats there

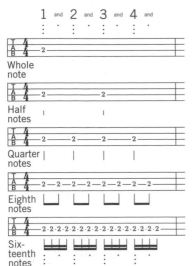

How the tab notations for whole-, half-, quarter-, eighth- and sixteenth-note durations relate to 4/4 time.

are in a bar (also known as a 'measure'). This is the way a musical score is divided up into equal sets of beats. The numbers in the time signature also tell you what type of note makes up each beat. We'll look at the time signature more in Week Five. For the moment, let's just stick with 4/4 time, which has four beats in a bar, each of which is a quarter note. Try playing the notes to the left while counting the numbers at the top. You'll have to count slowly to have any chance of plucking the sixteenth notes.

4. A ukulele instrumental

See if you can use your new-found tab skills to play 'Oh! Susanna' as an instrumental piece. Start off by playing just the melody, which is shown by the black tab notes. When you feel confident with this, you can try something a little fancier (and more difficult): hold the chord shapes as you pluck the melody and add in other notes from the chords here and there to give a fuller sound. Some suggested notes are in orange, but you could add any from the chords.

Oh! Susanna

The 2/2 time signature means there are two half notes per bar, so you count '1 and 2 and' for each bar.

The black and orange notes: First pluck the melody shown in black with your thumb. When you're happy with this, try adding the orange notes by holding down the chords. You can pluck the strings together like this:

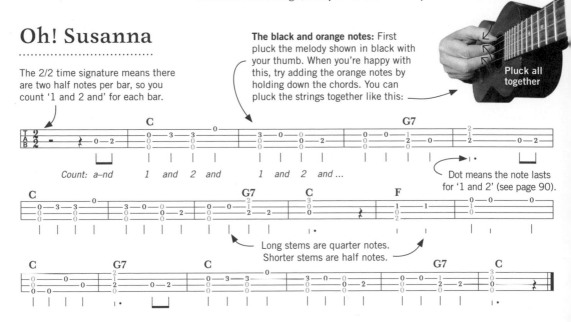

5. Practising

A tip to help you improve your playing, which applies during any of the weeks, is to record yourself. It is far easier to hear where you are going wrong and how you can improve when you are not so preoccupied trying to do everything at once.

Week Four

This week, we take a quick look at how to tune your ukulele to itself. Then we introduce the relaxed and syncopated calypso strum, and show how strums like this can be written down using slash notation. Finally, we break the great news that you need only four chords to play the vast majority of pop songs.

1. Tuning the uke to itself

As you saw in Week One, you end up having to tune your ukulele often. When you don't have an electronic tuner to hand and there isn't another available instrument that holds its tune (such as a keyboard) to tune your strings to, it is useful to be able to tune the ukulele to itself. This will mean that the strings are all in tune with each other, even if the 3rd string is not exactly tuned to a middle C. It won't be much use if you are playing with others or strumming along with a recording or video, but it works fine as a quick fix for those times when you're playing on your own.

Since you are tuning the strings to each other, this method isn't much help unless your uke is roughly in the right tuning ballpark. If your uke was in tune not so long ago, then it is worth using this method to get the strings sounding right together again. If you are tuning it for the first time, this is not the method for you.

You start by assuming the 3rd string is near enough to middle C, then use this to tune the 2nd string. That one is then used to tune both the 1st and the 4th strings. Here are the four steps:

STEP ONE	**STEP TWO**	**STEP THREE**	**STEP FOUR**
If the uke was in tune not so long ago, you should leave the 3rd string as it is and assume that it is not far off the middle C note that it should be. If the uke is nowhere near in tune, you are going to have to use one of the alternative tuning methods on page 82.	Compare the note of the open 2nd string (which is the E string) with an E played on the 3rd string, which you do by holding it down at the 4th fret. As always with tuning a stringed instrument, it is easier to start with the note too low and tune up.	Now compare the 1st string, which is the A string, to an A on the string you just finished tuning. An A is played on the 2nd string by holding it down at the 5th fret.	Finally, tune the 4th string, which is the g string. You can find a g on one of the other strings by holding down the 2nd string at the 3rd fret. As with all these tunings, you can sometimes hear a faint throbbing of the volume as the notes approach. This slows down as they become in tune.

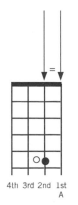

Some fretboards have a marker to show where the 5th fret is.

4th 3rd 2nd 1st
C

4th 3rd 2nd 1st
E

4th 3rd 2nd 1st
A

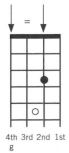

4th 3rd 2nd 1st
g

2. The calypso strum

Back in Week Two you learned three basic strumming patterns: the straight shuffle, the jazz shuffle and the church lick. Now it is time to add a fourth to your strummertoire: the calypso. It has a laid-back, syncopated feel, which is all very well for making it sound nicely Caribbean, but explaining how to do it on paper makes it look more complicated than it actually is.

The best approach, as ever, is to get a metronome or metronome app and slow it right down to help you count four beats in a bar. You'll need to count the 'ands' between the beats. On some counts, your strumming hand passes over the strings without touching them. On others, the beat is emphasized by strumming a little harder. You could do this with any strumming fingers, but it makes sense to use a combination of thumb and forefinger since sometimes you are emphasizing the downstroke and at other times the upstroke. Try it while holding down a C chord.

(Below) The calypso strum requires moving your hand down on each beat, and up on each half beat.

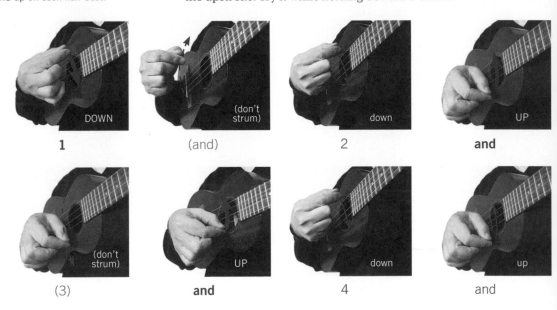

In fact, the up-and-down movements of your strumming hand are steady, without syncopation. The hand goes down on every beat, and up on each 'and' between the beats, just like the straight shuffle on page 89. The syncopation comes from the fact that you skip actually strumming the strings on a couple of the counts, and add emphasis on others. If you are finding it hard to work out how it should sound, it is well worth going online to watch a video of someone playing the calypso strum. When it comes to more complex rhythms, it is often easier just to copy someone doing it.

3. Slash notation for the calypso strum

As you have seen in previous weeks, strums are often written using slash notation. In Week Two, you saw that dots can be used to write out the syncopated feeling jazz shuffle (see page 90). In order to write the calypso strum in slash notation, a 'tie' is used to join two beats together. Here is how it looks:

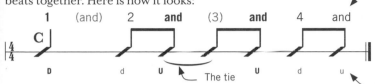

This shows what you count. The grey ones are not strummed. The red ones have emphasis.

The equivalent in tablature looks like this:

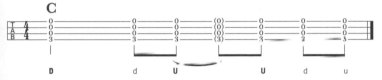

These letters signify whether you strum up or down. Capitals mean that the stroke should have emphasis.

The 4/4 time signature at the beginning shows that a bar is made up of four quarter notes (counted as 1, 2, 3, 4). This is the equivalent of eight eighth notes (counted as 1 and 2 and 3 and 4 and). The tie joins together two of these eighth notes. Rather than strumming them both, you skip the second strum and just hold the chord. It therefore lasts the length of two eighth notes, or a quarter note.

This is a quarter note in slash notation:

This is an eighth note in slash notation:

A quarter note sounds exactly the same as two eighth notes joined with a tie:

The calypso strum features heavily in this week's song, 'The Banana Boat Song' (see overleaf).

4. The universal four-chord song

You may have noticed that the songs you've played each week so far have used the same chords: C, F and G7. This week's 'Banana Boat Song' is no exception. You've already seen that these chords, along with Am, Em and Dm, which you have learned so far, are all part of the C family of chords. This means that they are all made up of notes from the C major scale, so they all sound good together. In fact, the first four that you learned, the C, F, G7 and Am, sound so good together that this combination of chords has become somewhat of a pop music cliché. You hear that chord progression all over the charts because it has instant appeal.

But it is the relationship between the chords that matters more than the chords themselves. These are the magic ones from the chord of C because they are the chords whose root notes are the first (C), fourth (F), fifth (G) and sixth (A) notes of the C major scale. In the key of F, the chords would be F, B♭, C7 and Dm, which are the equivalent chords whose roots are the first, fourth, fifth and sixth

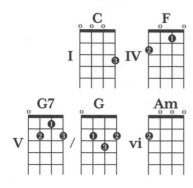

notes of the scale of F major. Since it is the gaps between the chord roots that matter, chord progressions like this are often referred to as numbers from the scale. The convention is to use Roman numerals (with minor chords written in lower case). The magic progression, which always sounds easy on the ear, is therefore using the chords I, IV, V and vi.

These chords for the key of C all happen to be easy to play on ukes with g, C, E, A tuning, which is why you've learned them first. In some pop songs, the V chord is played as a seventh chord, like G7, but often it is played as a major, like G (see page 109 for more about chord types). Using these chords, you can play all the songs listed below, and thousands more. It is really good practice for your ear to try working out the songs from these fragments (but bear in mind that the originals might not have been recorded in the key of C).

'Three Little Birds' *by Bob Marley*	The chorus chords are simply C and then F. In the verse, you start with C, change to G and back and then go to F …
'With or Without You' *by U2*	For both the verse and the chorus, the chord progression goes from C to G to Am and to F, before coming back to C …
'Let it Be' *by the Beatles*	The chords in the verse initially go from C to G to Am and to F. Then, like in the chorus, the progression is simply C to G to F and back to C …
'I Fought the Law' *covered by the Clash*	In the verse, it's C to F and back a couple of times before going from C to G and back. In the chorus, play F to C a few times and then it's like the verse …
'Hound Dog' *by Elvis Presley*	This '12-bar blues' progression is the same throughout the whole song. It goes from C to F and back and then to G7 and back.
'Brown Eyed Girl' *by Van Morrison*	The verse chords progress from C to F to C to G. In the chorus, they start with F and then go to G and C, followed by Am, F, G and C again.
'Ring of Fire' *played by Johnny Cash*	It's C to F to C in the verse, followed by C to G to C. In the chorus, the changes are G, F, C a couple of times before just C to F a couple of times.
'Hallelujah' *by Leonard Cohen*	There are quite a few changes in this one. In the verse it's C, Am, C, Am, F, G, C, G and then C, F, G, Am, F, G, Em, Am. The chorus is F, Am, F, C, G, C.

All you need are the same four simple chords to play thousands of pop songs, including those above. In the case of 'Hallelujah', you need this other C-family chord too:

Yes, OK, the last one was a cheat because it used Em too, but the lyrics in the first verse sum up the chord progression too well to miss.

5. Putting your calypso strum to use

The 'Banana Boat Song' is perfect for using your new strumming pattern. You can keep the same strum throughout except those bars where there's a chord change halfway through. The red slashes are just to alert you to where the chords change.

At first, it can feel like quite a challenge to strum one rhythm as you sing a slightly different one. Try getting the strumming right (counting 1-and-2-and … etc.) before you start the singing.

The Banana Boat Song

First note: Start singing with an E, which is the open 2nd string:

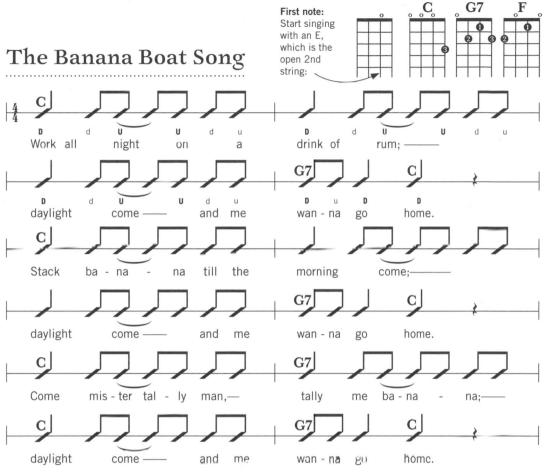

Work all night on a drink of rum; ——— daylight come ——— and me wan-na go home.

Stack ba-na-na till the morning come; ——— daylight come ——— and me wan-na go home.

Come mis-ter tal-ly man,— tally me ba-na-na;— daylight come ——— and me wan-na go home.

(Repeat from 'Come mister tally man ...' to '... wanna go home')

Lift (C) six foot, seven foot, eight foot bunch; daylight come and me (G7) wanna go (C) home.
(C) Six foot, seven foot, eight foot bunch; daylight come and me (G7) wanna go (C) home.

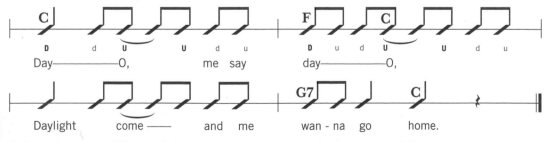

Day———O, me say day———O,

Daylight come ——— and me wan-na go home.

(C) Day–O, me say (F) day– (C) O; daylight come and me (G7) wanna go (C) home.

Week Five

It is time for some new chords. We will learn the ones in the G family, which will mean mastering the slightly tricky 'barre' chords. We'll get used to the waltzy feel of the 3/4 time signature, as well as learning how to make your chords sound classy with fingerpicking patterns.

(Above) The G chord is similar to G7, but with the 2nd string held down at the 3rd fret, rather than the 1st.

1. The G family and barre chords

Closely related to the C family, the G chord family includes some of the chords you have already learned from the C family. The root chord is G major, which you used in passing on page 100, and which differs from G7 by only one note. You therefore already know four of the six chords in the G family:

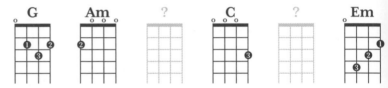

The bad news is that the two new ones are 'barre' chords, which are a little more fiddly. Barre chords involve using the same finger to press down on more than one string. Rather than the fingertip, the flat part of the finger is held across the strings being played. The convention is to write this on the chord diagram using a tie across all the strings that are held in the barre. Here, for instance, is one of the two new chords from the G family, called D7:

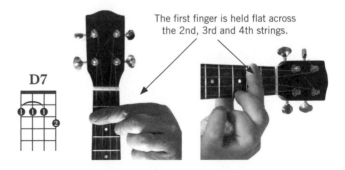

The first finger is held flat across the 2nd, 3rd and 4th strings.

One reason why barre chords like this are a little more difficult is because you can have to apply quite a bit of pressure on the barre finger to hold down all the strings. You will notice this more if your ukulele does not have a good 'action', which is related to how close the strings are to the fretboard (see page 80). Often, cheaper ukes have strings that are quite high off the fretboard, which means you have to press them down a lot to connect with the fret, compared to a uke with a good action, where the strings are close to the fretboard. The pressure on the barre finger needs to be even across all three strings it is holding down so that they are all held against the 2nd fret. As when learning any new chord, try playing each of the strings in turn to make sure that they are all producing clean notes. In the same way you fret an individual string, the barre finger should always be holding the strings just behind the 2nd fret, which means close to the fret but on the side away from the sound hole. If the strings sound buzzy, it is likely to be either because you have not positioned your barre finger correctly or because you are not pressing firmly and evenly enough across all three strings.

The other barre chord, which completes the G family, is B minor, or Bm. The barre is also made with the first finger at the 2nd fret, but this time it is the 1st, 2nd and 3rd strings that are fretted:

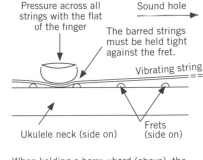

Pressure across all strings with the flat of the finger

Sound hole

The barred strings must be held tight against the fret.

Vibrating string

Ukulele neck (side on)

Frets (side on)

When holding a barre chord (above), the position of the finger relative to the fret is particularly critical for a clean sound. You need to hold down the strings just behind the fret (away from the sound hole) so that it acts as the fixed end point of the vibrating string.

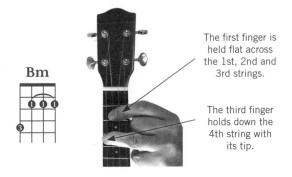

Bm

The first finger is held flat across the 1st, 2nd and 3rd strings.

The third finger holds down the 4th string with its tip.

2. Fingerpicking chords

In Week Three you saw how to read tablature to play a melody on your uke, picking individual strings to play it as a solo instrument. Fingerpicking, just like strumming, can also be used to accompany your singing. You hold the chords of the song as normal but, rather than strumming them, you use your different fingers to pick each of the strings in turn. This technique is well worth perfecting, not least because it sounds really classy, yet is not particularly difficult to play.

The first trick is to assign the fingers of your strumming hand – which is now your picking hand – to each of the four strings of the uke. You can start by resting each finger on its string. In our first arrangement, the thumb goes on the 4th string (the one nearest you), your first finger on the 3rd string, your second finger on the 2nd string and your third finger on the 1st string (see right). This is the arrangement that works best for the up-and-down fingerpicking pattern.

4th string
3rd string
2nd string
1st string

It is important for each of your fingers to know its place.

When you first practise fingerpicking, it is a good idea simply to deaden the strings with your fretting hand. In other words, don't actually press down on the strings to hold them to the fretboard. Instead, just hold your fingers against them to dampen them so that you can concentrate on plucking the strings with your other hand without worrying about the notes.

You are going to start by plucking each of the strings with each of your fingers, starting with the thumb on the 4th string and ending with your third finger on the 1st string. Written in tab, it might look as shown below (there are Xs on the tab rather than numbers because you are deadening the strings, rather than fretting them):

This tab has Xs in place of numbers because you are deadening the strings (to practise plucking), so you are not holding them down at any fret (which is what numbers on a tab refer to).

These are not to do with counting, but show which fingers you should be using to pluck the strings.

As you pluck the strings, your hand should feel relaxed. As always, you will be gripping the ukulele against your chest with the inside of the picking forearm. Your thumb plucks downwards on the 4th string, while each of your first, second and third fingers pluck upwards on their strings. Your thumb should be forward of the other fingers – more towards the neck of the ukulele – so that it feels as if each of your other fingers is pulling in towards your palm as it plucks the string.

Thumb plucks down forward of the other fingers (towards the neck). The other fingers pluck in towards the palm.

Unlike when you are strumming, your hand should not be moving up or down at all. It should just hang there, as relaxed as you can make it, while the fingers pluck. Fingerpicking can feel a little uncomfortable when you are not used to the movements, but it is well worth persevering with the technique because it sounds great once you start holding chords with your other hand instead of just deadening the strings.

When you feel reasonably comfortable with the finger movements and you can pick each of the strings in turn with just small movements of the fingers while the body of your hand remains pretty stationary, it is time to start introducing some chords to your picking. Try picking the strings as previously described while you hold a G chord. Then see if you can change to a D7 (the numbers refer to the fret to be held):

Remember, the lines on tablature refer to the strings of your uke, while the numbers tell you the fret at which to hold the string down.

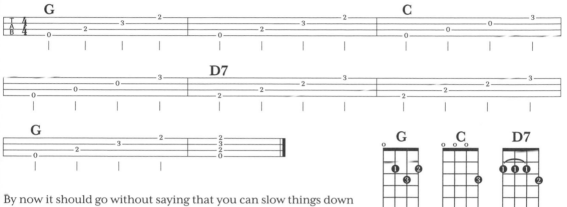

By now it should go without saying that you can slow things down if necessary to help you change the chords without slowing the pace of your fingerpicking. Since the D7 is a barre chord, you will need to really press down with the first finger barre in the right place to make sure that all the notes sound clean. In this regard, fingerpicking is less forgiving of poorly fretted chords than strumming is. Or, to put it another way, the great thing about fingerpicking chords is that you are forced to adjust your chord position until all the notes sound good.

3. Shifting to 3/4 time for the song

You are going to use fingerpicking chords to accompany this week's song, but with a slightly different picking pattern. This time, having picked from the 4th string to the 1st, you will come back again. It's a sort of up-and-down picking pattern. While the hand movements are no more complicated, this does mean playing to a different time signature. In 3/4 time, there are not four beats in every bar, as has been the case in all the songs you have played so far, but three. This is the old waltz rhythm, where you count only 1, 2, 3 ... to get the song started.

Try strumming the pattern shown in slash notation to the right. Just deaden the strings with your fretting hand and make each stroke with short downward strums. This will be the rhythm of your up-and-down fingerpicking pattern. Now try the same rhythm by picking the strings (also deadened) in the tab overleaf. Remember, the numbers beneath show which fingers to pick with.

The 3/4 time signature tells you that there are three beats of quarter-note duration in each bar. Here each of these has been broken into two eighth notes.

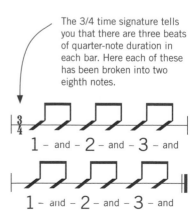

1 – and – 2 – and – 3 – and

1 – and – 2 – and – 3 – and

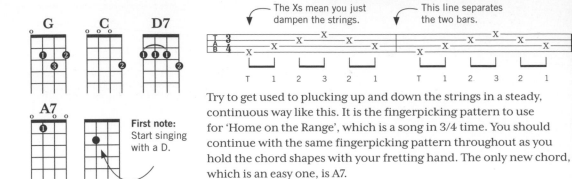

The Xs mean you just dampen the strings.

This line separates the two bars.

Try to get used to plucking up and down the strings in a steady, continuous way like this. It is the fingerpicking pattern to use for 'Home on the Range', which is a song in 3/4 time. You should continue with the same fingerpicking pattern throughout as you hold the chord shapes with your fretting hand. The only new chord, which is an easy one, is A7.

First note: Start singing with a D.

Home on the Range

Changing between G, C and D7 will be easier if you play the C using your second finger (see the chord diagram above).

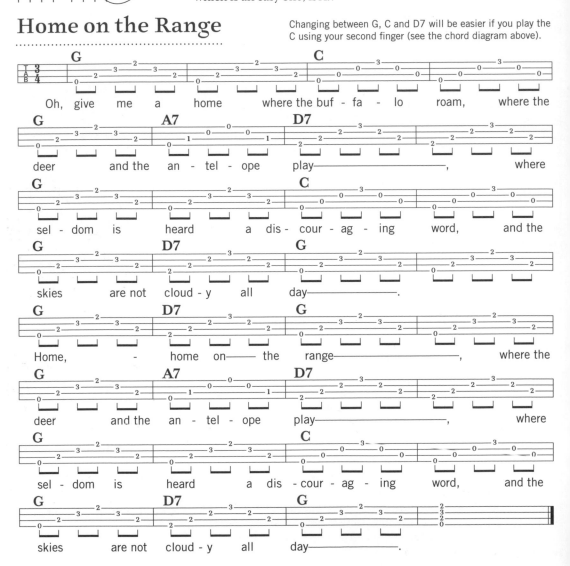

Week Six

In this final week, you will learn how to add colour and variety to your ukulele strumming with some fancy fingerwork known as the 'four-finger roll' and the 'triplet strum'. We will also explain how chords work so you'll be able to use the Chord Finder with confidence (see the inside covers).

1. Getting fancy: the four-finger roll

As well as being a melodic instrument, the ukulele is a rhythmic one. This is particularly apparent when the usual strums are supplemented with fancier hand movements known as 'rolls'.

A ukulele roll is when the up-and-down movements of your strumming hand over the strings are augmented by flicks of the strumming fingers. In other words, you are adding the independent movements of your fingers to the overall movement of your hand.

You already know about the overall hand movements as they're how you have been doing your strumming up to now. We'll start, therefore, with the finger movements. Later we can try adding them to the overall hand movements.

Start with your strumming hand held in a very loose fist about an inch above the strings. The fist should be so loose that your fingers aren't even touching your palm. You can just deaden the strings with your other hand as the notes are not important at this stage. Starting with your little (or fourth) finger, you are going to flick each finger out and across the strings in turn: your fourth, followed by your third, second and first should flick across the strings in turn. Your hand as a whole doesn't move downwards, it just gently swivels at the wrist as each finger opens out in turn. Don't worry about doing it fast. You just want to start getting used to the feeling of the four fingers flicking across the deadened strings in turn.

(Above) Here's a reminder of which number refers to which finger.

(Above) The four-finger roll starts with the strumming hand in a loose fist.

This four-finger roll won't feel like an easy movement because it is not something you usually ask your fingers to do – unless you happen to be a flamenco guitarist or an expert in traditional Indian dance. Try to make the succession of fingers strumming across the strings into a fluid and continuous movement, as if you are throwing open a Japanese fan.

(Above, left to right) As you play a four-finger roll, each finger, starting with your fourth and ending with your first, strums across the strings in quick succession.

When performing the four-finger roll (above), make sure your hand is angled so that the fingers strum downwards over the strings rather than diagonally. The hand naturally swivels at the wrist as the fingers extend.

The effectiveness of your fingers brushing across all the strings in close succession depends greatly on the position of your hand over the strings. If it is too close, at the wrong angle or too tense, the fingers will snag on the individual strings, rather than sweeping across all four strings. Try slightly different positions of the hand until you find the most effective one. The fingers should be sweeping downwards over the strings, rather than at an angle.

There should be a natural twisting of the wrist as the fingers are thrown out. As with all strumming, the best way to work out what your fingers should be doing is to watch someone else slowly doing a four-finger roll. The Internet is an invaluable tool for finding videos of how the more complicated strums and rolls should look and sound.

The more you practise this movement, the more natural it will feel. You don't even need your uke with you. When you have an idle moment at work, practise the four-finger roll against your outer trouser leg. Who cares what Maureen in Accounts thinks?

You will be pleased to learn that when you are playing ukulele rolls in real life, you don't need to perform them over and over like this. In fact, a roll works best by giving emphasis and colour to a particular beat within a strumming pattern. For instance, use it in place of the second stroke in the calypso strum that you learned back in Week Four. The tab below shows how the strum looked without any roll, and gives the counting to help you remember the rhythm. Begin by strumming it with your first (or index) finger.

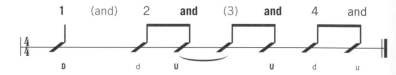

Now try replacing the second strum (the count marked '2') with a four-finger roll. Having thrown your fingers down with the roll, you can come back up again with the pad of your first finger on the 'and' count that follows the '2'. In slash notation, the four-finger roll can be represented by a wiggly arrow and the letter 'R' for *rasgueado*, which is the flamenco guitar term for rolls like this.

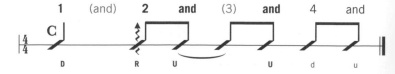

You'll need to practise to play the roll in place of the second downstroke without having to slow the pace of the calypso strum. As always, start doing it slowly and pick up the pace when you get used to it. Having made the downstroke on the count of '1', bring your fingers into the loose fist during the silent 'and' count, ready to make the roll on the count of '2'.

When you feel you have got the hang of it, go back to page 101 and try playing 'The Banana Boat Song' using this fancier calypso rhythm.

2. How chords work

The Chord Finder on the inside covers of this book shows most of the ukulele chords that you will ever need – certainly all the ones used in the Songbook. Once you know how to read chord diagrams, it is easy to work out how to play them, even if some have awkward positions that require practice for all the notes to sound clean. You've already come across major chords, which are written with a capital letter, such as 'C', and minor chords, written like 'Am', and the seventh chords, such as 'G7'. But what about all the other strange-looking names in the Chord Finder, such as 'B♭', 'F♯m7', 'Gaug' and 'Cdim'? It is not necessary to stress yourself out trying to learn them all by heart – you'll pick them up over time as you come across them in sheet music – but a little of the theory behind chords will help demystify the names and symbols.

WHAT IS A CHORD? A chord is just a group of three or more notes played together. The chord names can be thought of as having two parts. They always start with the name of a note. This is called the 'root' of the chord, and can be any one of the notes on a ukulele, as shown on the right. The root is the note upon which the chord is built, so is the most important note of the chord.

THE QUALITY OF A CHORD The second part of the chord name gives its 'quality' – whether it is major or minor, a 7th chord (such as G7) or some other type. It is nothing more than a shorthand way of saying which notes, in addition to the root, make up the chord.

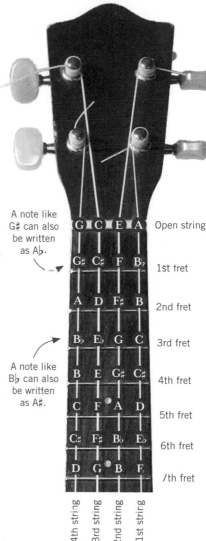

A note like G♯ can also be written as A♭.

A note like B♭ can also be written as A♯.

G	C	E	A	Open string
G♯	C♯	F	B♭	1st fret
A	D	F♯	B	2nd fret
B♭	E♭	G	C	3rd fret
B	E	G♯	C♯	4th fret
C	F	A	D	5th fret
C♯	F♯	B♭	E♭	6th fret
D	G	B	F	7th fret

4th string 3rd string 2nd string 1st string

The names of the notes on the first seven frets of a ukulele with g, C, E, A tuning (above). You can see that the same notes can be played on different strings. Notes that sound the same, one being a higher version of the other, are described as being an 'octave' apart, and also have the same name. C on the 3rd fret of the 1st string, for instance, is an octave above the C on the open 3rd string.

The **root** of this chord is the note B♭.

B♭m

The **quality** of this chord is minor.

When there is no part of the chord name after the root to specify the quality, the chord is assumed to be a major one. Whether the quality is implicit like this or is specified by one of the many abbreviations, such as '-m', '-7' and '-dim', the quality of the chord specifies the

Minor chords all consist of the root plus the notes one-and-a-half, and three-and-a-half steps above it (three and seven frets).

Major chords all consist of the root plus the notes two, and three-and-a-half steps above it (four and seven frets).

fixed, mathematical way that you count in steps up from the root to find the other notes that make up the chord. Each fret on the uke fretboard is a half step. So a whole step is always two frets. No matter which root the chord has as its fundamental note, the steps you count up to find the other notes for a certain quality of chord will always be the same. In other words, the gaps or 'intervals' between the notes are the same for all major chords, for all minor chords, and for all minor 7th (-m7) chords.

COMPONENTS OF A CHORD In the case of a major chord, there are three component notes: the root (of course), the note two steps above it (the same as four frets) and the note three-and-a-half steps above it (the same as seven frets). In the case of C major (which is just written as C), the notes are C, E and G. It doesn't matter where on the fretboard you find these notes: you could play a high C and a low E, with a G in between. You are used to playing C major with the 1st string held at the 3rd fret and the other strings open so that you sound the notes G, C, E and C as you strum downwards from the 4th to the 1st string. But you could hold these notes in other positions. Such alternative fingerings are called 'inversions' of the C chord. When you are strumming uke chords with someone else, the sound will be much richer if you sometimes play different inversions from each other.

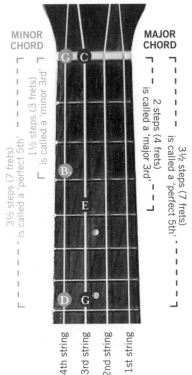

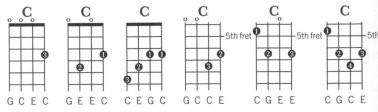

Six different ways of playing a C major chord, known as inversions. The three diagrams on the right show the fingering relative to the 5th fret.

All major and all minor chords consist of three notes, which always share exactly the same relationship with the root note of the chord. When you compare the pattern of a Gm chord and a C chord, you can see that the very contrasting major and minor types of chord differ only by the middle note being half a step, or one fret, out.

Although they feel slightly different from each other, these inversions are all C major because they all combine the notes C, E and G.

You need to change only one of the notes by half a step (one fret) to make a minor chord. Like major chords, minors contain the root and the note three-and-a-half steps (seven frets) above it. This time, however, the note in between is only one-and-a-half steps (three frets) above the root. As you can see on the left, the chord of Gm is therefore made of the notes G, B♭ and D. Again these notes can be combined in many different positions, giving different inversions. A seventh chord, such as G7, is made up of the three notes of the major chord (G, B and D), plus the note that is five steps (ten frets) above the root, which is F, an interval known in music as a 'minor 7th'.

The Chord Finder shows only one position for each chord, but in every case the chord is simply the root plus two or three additional notes that are a fixed number of steps away from it. As with major and minor chords, just a slight difference of the intervals between the notes that make up chords can give them completely different characters. Some feel bright, some melancholy, some beg to be resolved to other chords, some jar in a deliciously jazzy way. If you want to find alternative inversions of the chords and you have a smartphone, you could try one of the many uke-chord apps, which show several alternative positions, or inversions, for each chord.

3. The triplet strum

You've now reached almost the end of Week Six, with just one fancy strum left for you to master, so give yourself a pat on the back whilst performing a twiddly flourish of your strumming fingers.

The triplet strum is a really good one to learn as it will help you to sound and look like a ukulele expert. Thankfully, the finger movements are not as convoluted as the four-finger strum, but it takes some practice to incorporate triplets into your strumming so that the combination sounds fluid and continuous. Before worrying too much about that, let's just get the rhythm and finger movements right.

A triplet involves dividing one or more of the standard beats of a bar into three quick beats. Try strumming this rhythm (while just deadening the strings with your fretting hand) initially using simple downstrokes of your forefinger (first finger). The third of the four beats in the bar is broken into triplets. To get the timing of the beats right, it is worth thinking of each of the four beats in the bar being divided into three (giving the counting a waltz-like feel). Only when it comes to the third beat do you actually strum the triplets:

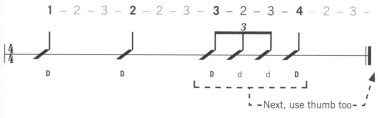

As always, start slowly. Once you have got the feel of the rhythm using downstrokes of your forefinger, try strumming the triplet using your forefinger, then thumb, then forefinger, as shown on the right. It is worth looking online for videos of triplet strums in action, but remember that some people use different fingers to make the triplets, so make sure you watch someone do it the way shown

The Basic Triplet Rhythm

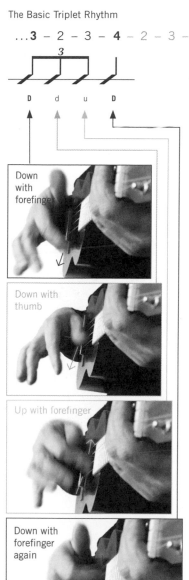

Down with forefinger

Down with thumb

Up with forefinger

Down with forefinger again

Once you have got used to playing a triplet with just your forefinger, try doing it as shown above with your finger and thumb. With practice, this way will enable you to play triplets much faster.

Down by the Riverside

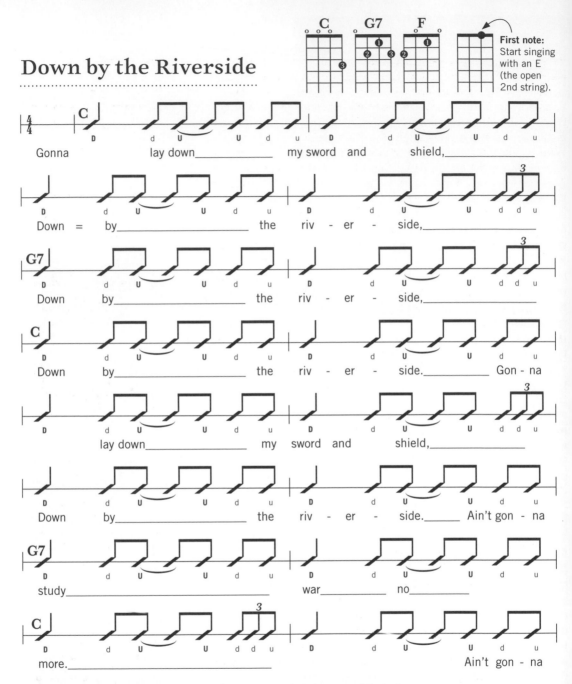

(F) study war no more.
I ain't gonna (C) study war no more,
(G7) Study war no (C) more.

I ain't gonna (F) study war no more.
I ain't gonna (C) study war no more,
(G7) Study war no (C) more.

(Repeat from beginning)

here. Your challenge is to incorporate the triplet without breaking the rhythm of the strumming. The overall up and down of your hand as you strum down on the main beats of the bar should not be interrupted as you throw in the remaining two triplets between the third and fourth strums. Following the downstroke on the third main beat of the bar, it should feel as if you are leaving your thumb behind when your hand moves down with the forefinger strum, only for it to catch up again by strumming down before strumming up again with the forefinger. As you get more used to it, you can try throwing in the triplet on any one of the four main beats in the bar.

The song for this, your final week, is the old gospel song 'Down by the Riverside', shown opposite. If you can't remember how it goes, you could start by listening online to the version that Mahalia Jackson sang. The chords are C, G7 and F, which will be very familiar to you by now. You'll see from the slash notation that the strumming pattern is the calypso strum, which you first encountered in Week Four (see page 98). We have also thrown in a few triplet strums to spice things up. The combination is not easy and will take some practice, not least because the triplet strums tend to happen just before a chord change.

Start by playing the song without trying to put in any triplets. Just practise until you feel happy with playing the normal calypso strum throughout. Then you can start trying to add in the triplets where shown. They end up replacing the last two strokes of the calypso pattern, so rather than ending the bar with down-up, you end it with down-down-up. You have to change quickly between the C and G7 chords after the triplet, so remember to keep your third finger on the 1st string and slide it along a fret to make the change.

4. Where do you go from here?

Your ukulele playing will improve most if you practise little and often, and just like picking up a new language, the best way to become fluent is through imitation. Make use of the enormous wealth of uke videos online (see page 138). If you like something, try to copy it.

As you work through the songs in the rest of this book, experiment with how you play them. Each arrangement is just one way of playing the song. Try different strums and alternative inversions of the chords. Try slowing a song right down until it sounds completely different. The more you experiment, the more flexible your playing will become. Develop your own style.

And finally, don't just play on your own, join a uke club. If there isn't one near you, start your own. This beautiful little instrument, born out of the *aloha* spirit of the Hawaiian Islands, was always meant to be shared.

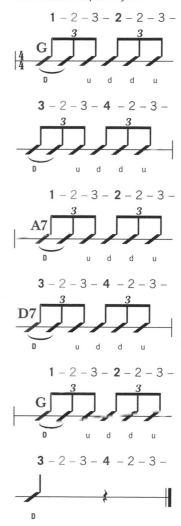

The Hawaiian Triplet Rhythm

The triplet strum (above) features heavily in Hawaiian ukulele music, where it tends to be combined with a swing beat similar to the jazz shuffle described on page 90. If you have difficulty working out the rhythm above, listen for it online in a traditional rendition of the classic Hawaiian song, 'Alekoki'. (Look in the Chord Finder on the inside covers if you need reminding about how to hold the chords.)

How to Change Your Uke Strings

New strings on your ukulele every few months make a huge difference.

THE THOUGHT of changing the strings on your ukulele can seem a little daunting at first. How do you tie the string on? Which way should it wind around the tuning pegs? How do you bring it up to the right tension? Don't worry. It really isn't a big deal once you know how.

But why bother changing your strings in the first place? If you have a fairly cheap ukulele, it probably came with inferior strings. Adding good new ones will not only improve the sound, but will probably also help it to stay in tune for longer. Whatever uke you have, it is worth changing your strings every three to six months, depending on how much you are playing it. This is because, over time, the strings wear against the saddle, nut and frets and are no longer of even thickness. As a result, the instrument is harder to tune and the notes do not sound as pure and bright as they should. Change strings also if you are after a different tone. Some types give a warm note, while others have a brighter, punchier sound.

CHOOSING THE RIGHT STRINGS

1. Select the right size. There are different sets of strings for different size ukes. The choice depends on how long the strings are and, more importantly, how much tension is needed to get them in tune. Small ukes are often not strong enough to take high-tension strings, so make sure you buy strings that match your type of uke (see page 78 for more about sizes).

2. Choose the string material. Forget the old 'catgut' strings. They were actually made from the guts of sheep or goats, and while they had a rich sound, they didn't last long and went out of tune easily with changes in humidity and temperature. Modern strings are much more stable and come in three basic materials: nylon (a slightly warm sound), fluorocarbon (bright and punchy) and Nylgut® (close to the original gut sound, but louder). Try different types over time to see which you prefer. Two good brands to start with are Aquila, made of Nylgut®, and Worth, made of fluorocarbon. Banjoleles can be strung with standard uke strings or (like regular banjos) with steel strings for a louder, twangier sound. Never put steel strings on a ukulele. It isn't designed to withstand their higher tension, and will warp or crack. If you are lucky enough to have a very old soprano uke, look for light-tension strings (nylon or fluorocarbon). Old ukes weren't designed to stand up to high-tension modern strings.

3. Buy strings for your tuning. The choice depends on whether or not you use re-entrant tuning, which this book recommends (see page 82). This tuning means that the 4th string (nearest your head) has a higher note than the 3rd. Strings

Early ukulele strings, such as the Melody and Perfecto brands, were made of animal intestines. Modern alternative materials include fluorocarbon (used for Worth strings) and Nylgut® (developed by Aquila).

for this tuning are labelled as 'standard tuning' or with the notes 'g, C, E, A'. If you want to be able to play bass notes (perhaps to accompany a standard-tuned uke) on a tenor or baritone ukulele, you can try tuning it with the 4th string an octave below: to a low G. This needs a string made of wire wound around nylon. Strings for this tuning are generally described as 'Low G' or 'G, C, E, A'. They're appropriate only for tenor or baritone ukes as the tension of the 4th string would damage a soprano or concert uke.

RE-STRINGING YOUR UKULELE

1. **Replace strings one at a time** so that the changes in tension are less traumatic for your little instrument. Start with the 4th string (the one nearest your head as you play the uke).
2. **Take off the old string** by unwinding the tuning key until it is loose, then unravel the string from the tuning peg and untie it from the bridge. As you do so, pay attention to how the string was tied.
3. **Select the correct string from the set**. Things will go pear-shaped if you put the strings on in the wrong order, so pay attention to what is written on the sleeves before you take the strings out. Remember, when you are holding the uke to play it, the 1st string is nearest the floor and the 4th string is nearest your head.
4. **Attach one end of the string to the bridge.** There are two systems for this, depending on whether you have a slotted or a tie-on bridge (see above right). Slotted is easy: just tie a knot in the string (a double one if it is thin, compared to the slot) and slip it in so that it holds. Tie-on bridges are more fiddly. Follow the diagram to the right.
5. **Attach the string to the tuning peg.** Feed it around the top of the peg (see the diagram, right, for the correct direction) and through the hole. Take up the slack (ensuring that the string is sitting in the right groove of the nut) and wind it two or three times around the peg before feeding it through the hole again. This will help stop the string from slipping under tension.
6. **Tighten the string.** This can take a lot of winding of the tuning key. Get it into the right tuning ballpark by comparing the note to one of the other strings (see page 97). Until it settles down, the string will keep going out of tune as it stretches. Try holding the string near the sound hole and vigorously wiggling it up and down in between tuning to aid the stretching process. Once it is not going out of tune so much, move on to changing the next string along.
7. **Keep tuning and stretching.** After changing the strings, you will find that they keep going out of tune. Even with wiggling, the strings stretch, but eventually settle down and hold their tune. Just be prepared to do more tuning than normal and keep wiggling the strings to speed them along. An electronic tuner (see page 82) is more helpful than ever when you are running in new strings like this.

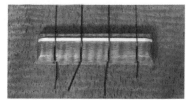

Slotted bridge: Tie a knot and slip the string into the slot so that it holds.

Might need a double knot.

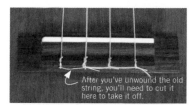

After you've unwound the old string, you'll need to cut it here to take it off.

Tie-on bridge: Start with the 4th string and tuck the tail of each under the loop of the next string.

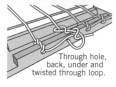

Through hole, back, under and twisted through loop.

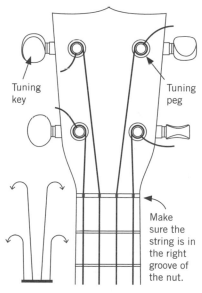

Tuning key

Tuning peg

Make sure the string is in the right groove of the nut.

Think of a water fountain (above left) to remember which way the strings should wind around the tuning pegs.

Songbook

Man of Constant Sorrow

Folk traditional

Bob Dylan recorded this great old bluesy folk song for his debut album, released in 1962. It was first recorded by singer Dick Burnett around 1913. Folk song archivist Cecil Sharp printed a version in 1918, titled 'In Old Virginny'. It came to public attention again when a version was included in the 2000 Coen brothers film *O Brother, Where Art Thou?*, starring George Clooney.

Chord diagrams

F F7 B♭ C7

First note: Start singing with the note C, played on the 1st string at the 3rd fret.

Strumming

A normal straight shuffle (see page 89) should do the trick, but you want the down- and upstrokes to feel quite fast. It should sound like the chugga-chugga-chugga of a train powering across the prairies of the US Midwest.

      F   F7   B♭
1. I am a man of constant sorrow.

            C7   F
I have seen trouble all my days.

         F7   B♭
I bid farewell to old Kentucky,

              C7   F
The state where I was born and raised.

2. (F) For six long (F7) years I've been in (B♭) trouble;
No pleasure (C7) here on earth, I've (F) found.
(F) For in this (F7) world I'm bound to (B♭) travel.
I have no (C7) friends to help me (F) now.

3. (F) You may (F7) bury me in some deep (B♭) valley;
For many (C7) years where I may (F) lay.
(F) Then you may (F7) learn to love (B♭) another
While I am (C7) sleeping in my (F) grave.

4. (F) Maybe your (F7) friends think I'm just a (B♭) stranger;
My face you'll (C7) never see no (F) more.
(F) But there is one (F7) promise that is (B♭) given:
I'll meet you (C7) on God's golden (F) shore.

Drunken Sailor

Folk traditional

This is probably the best singalong sea shanty ever composed, originally conceived for sailors to sing when hauling in a rope. Some scholars contend that the 'earl-eye' pronunciation was a later affectation, so we've left it out. You might want to make up your own sobering punishments for the drunken sailor.

Chord diagrams

Am **G**

First note: Start singing with the note E, which is the open 2nd string.

Strumming

You could try a strumming style that mirrors the singing rhythm of the first line. This is shown below in rhythm notation (see page 90). Emphasizing the down-up strums on the 2nd and 4th beat gives the strumming a sea shanty feel. Strum with a little more force on these strokes, which are marked in red.

Count:	1 – (and) – **2** – **and** – 3 – (and) – **4** – **and**	– 1 – (and) – **2** – **and** – 3 – (and) – **4** – **and** –
Strum:	d – – D – U – d – – D – U	– d – – D – U – d – – D – U
Sing:	What shall we do with a drun – ken sai – lor?	

Am
1. What shall we do with a drunken sailor?

G
What shall we do with a drunken sailor?

Am
What shall we do with a drunken sailor?

     G   **Am**
Early in the morning!

Am
Chorus: *Hooray and up she rises,*

G
Hooray and up she rises,

Am
Hooray and up she rises,

    G   **Am**
Early in the morning.

2. (**Am**) Put him in a longboat till he's sober ... (*x3*)
Early (**G**) in the (**Am**) morning!
Chorus

3. (**Am**) Pull out the plug and wet him all over ... (*x3*)
Early (**G**) in the (**Am**) morning!
Chorus

4. (**Am**) Put him in the bilge and make him drink
   it ... (*x3*)
Early (**G**) in the (**Am**) morning!
Chorus

5. (**Am**) Shave his belly with a rusty razor ... (*x3*)
Early (**G**) in the (**Am**) morning!
Chorus

6. (**Am**) Heave him by the leg with a running
   bowline ... (*x3*)
Early (**G**) in the (**Am**) morning!
Chorus

7. (**Am**) That's what we do with a drunken sailor ... (*x3*)
Early (**G**) in the (**Am**) morning!
Chorus

Scarborough Fair

Folk traditional

This lovely medieval ballad is a must for your uke repertoire. If singing in mixed company, give the first four verses to the men and the rest to the women. Each asks impossible tasks of the other: he asks his former true love to make a shirt without a seam and to wash it in a dry well. She responds by asking him to shear a field with a sickle of leather and bind it with a peacock feather.

     Dm   C   Dm
1. Are you going to Scarborough Fair?

                         G   Dm
Parsley, sage, rosemary and thyme;

                F   C
Remember me to one who lives there,

Dm   C   Dm
She once was a true love of mine.

2. (Dm) Tell her to make me a (C) cambric (Dm) shirt,
Parsley, sage, rose-(G)mary and (Dm) thyme;
Without a (F) seam or needle-(C)work,
(Dm) She will (C) be a true love of (Dm) mine.

3. (Dm) Tell her to wash it in (C) yonder dry (Dm) well,
Parsley, sage, rose-(G)mary and (Dm) thyme;
Where never spring (F) water or rain ever (C) fell,
(Dm) She will (C) be a true love of (Dm) mine.

4. (Dm) Tell her to dry it on (C) yonder grey (Dm) thorn,
Parsley, sage, rose-(G)mary and (Dm) thyme;
Which never bore (F) blossom since Adam was (C) born,
(Dm) She will (C) be a true love of (Dm) mine.

5. (Dm) Now he has (C) asked me questions (Dm) three,
Parsley, sage, rose-(G)mary and (Dm) thyme;
I hope he'll (F) answer as many for (C) me
(Dm) Before he (C) shall be a true love of (Dm) mine.

6. (Dm) Tell him to (C) buy me an acre of (Dm) land,
Parsley, sage, rose-(G)mary and (Dm) thyme;
Betwixt the salt (F) water and the sea (C) sand,
(Dm) Then he (C) shall be a true love of (Dm) mine.

Chord diagrams

First note: Start singing with the note D, played on the 3rd string at the 2nd fret.

Strumming

This song is in 3/4 time, which means that you count in at the beginning with '1, 2, 3 ...' and each bar has three beats in it. For instance, the first word, 'Are', lasts for two beats and the second word, 'you', lasts for one.

This has an impact on the sort of strumming pattern you should use. You could simply strum down once on each beat so that you strum down twice as you sing 'Are', and a third time as you sing 'you'. Alternatively, you could try a strumming pattern like the one shown below (see page 90 for more on rhythm notation).

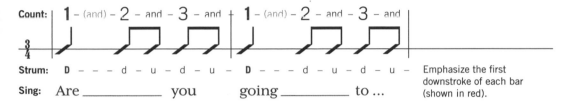

Emphasize the first downstroke of each bar (shown in red).

7. **(Dm)** Tell him to **(C)** plough it with a ram's **(Dm)** horn,
Parsley, sage, rose-**(G)**mary and **(Dm)** thyme;
And sow it all **(F)** over with one pepper-**(C)**corn,
(Dm) And he **(C)** shall be a true love of **(Dm)** mine.

8. **(Dm)** Tell him to **(C)** shear it with a sickle of **(Dm)** leather,
Parsley, sage, rose-**(G)**mary and **(Dm)** thyme;
And bind it **(F)** up with a peacock **(C)** feather,
(Dm) And he **(C)** shall be a true love of **(Dm)** mine.

9. **(Dm)** Tell him to **(C)** thrash it on yonder **(Dm)** wall,
Parsley, sage, rose-**(G)**mary and **(Dm)** thyme;
And never let **(F)** one corn of it **(C)** fall,
(Dm) Then he **(C)** shall be a true love of **(Dm)** mine.

10. **(Dm)** When he has **(C)** done and finished his **(Dm)** work,
Parsley, sage, rose-**(G)**mary and **(Dm)** thyme;
Oh, tell him to **(F)** come and he'll have his **(C)** shirt,
(Dm) And he **(C)** shall be a true love of **(Dm)** mine.

Aloha Oe

Words and music by Queen Lili'uokalani

This is the most famous of all Hawaiian songs. To help you learn the singing melody, we've included ukulele tablature (see pages 92 and 95) – and also the Hawaiian lyrics in case these have slipped your mind.

Chord diagrams

Strumming

First note: Start singing with the note D, played on the 3rd string at the 2nd fret.

You could just strum downwards in a relaxed, languid fashion on each of the four beats of every bar. Alternatively, you could try the rather more challenging Hawaiian triplet strum (see page 111). This means you play four triplets within each bar, so is best attempted when you have got the hang of those. The counting for this rhythm is on page 113.

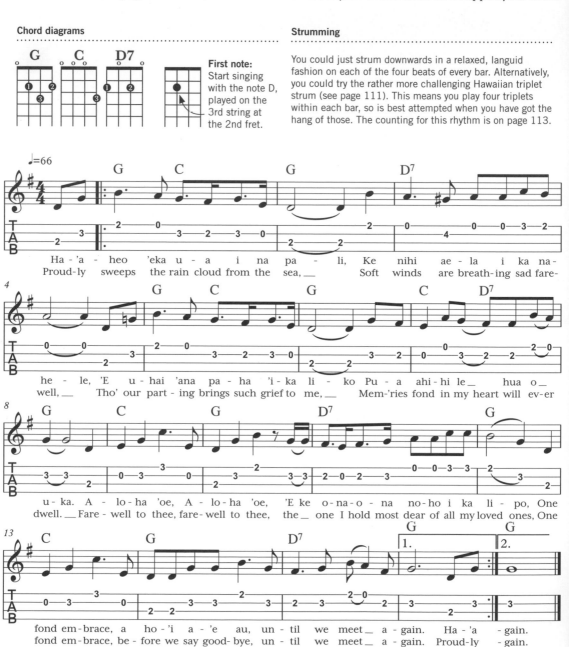

Ha-'a-heo 'eka u-a i na pa-li, Ke nihi ae-la i ka na-
Proud-ly sweeps the rain cloud from the sea, __ Soft winds are breath-ing sad fare-

he-le, 'E u-hai 'ana pa-ha 'i-ka li-ko Pu-a ahi-hi le __ hua o __
well, __ Tho' our part-ing brings such grief to me, __ Mem-'ries fond in my heart will ev-er

u-ka. A-lo-ha 'oe, A-lo-ha 'oe, 'E ke o-na-o-na no-ho i ka li-po, One
dwell. __ Fare-well to thee, fare-well to thee, the __ one I hold most dear of all my loved ones, One

fond em-brace, a ho-'i a-'e au, un-til we meet __ a-gain. Ha-'a - gain.
fond em-brace, be-fore we say good-bye, un-til we meet __ a-gain. Proud-ly - gain.

By the Light of the Silvery Moon

Music by Gus Edwards
Words by Edward Madden

This Tin Pan Alley classic was written in 1909 and is just the song for some moonlit serenading. Besides the essential chords, we've included some optional, more challenging ones, shown in a paler colour within the lyrics, which add a deliciously jazzy feel. As these make the chord changes a little swift, you might want to add them once you are confident with the basic progression.

Essential chords

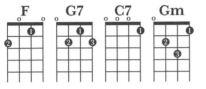

Optional jazzy chords

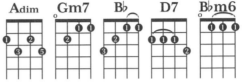

First note: Start singing with an A, which is the open 1st string.

Strumming

This song is in 4/4 time, which means that each bar has four beats in it. You can simply strum a downstroke on each beat, as shown below.

In general, try to make the strums sound short, but if you play the optional jazzy chords, try to hold and strum them in a more lingering way.

Count: 1 - 2 - 3 - 4 - 1 - 2 - 3 - 4 - 1 - 2 - 3 - 4 - 1 - 2 - 3 - 4 -
Strum: d – d – d – d – d – d – d – d – d – d – d – d – d – d – d – d –
Sing: By the light ——————— of the silvery moon, ————

          F   G7
By the light of the silvery moon,

            C7
I want to spoon.

                       F   Adim Gm7 C7
To my honey, I'll croon love's tune.

          F   Bb   D7 Gm
Honeymoon keep a-shining in June.

          Bbm6 F   Bbm6   F
Your silvery beams will bring love dreams.

                    G7   Gm7
We'll be cuddling soon,

            C7   F   Gm7 C7 F
By the silvery moon.

(Repeat)

The House of the Rising Sun

Folk traditional

The British pop group The Animals had their breakthrough hit in 1964 with their own arrangement of this old American folk song. Here we reproduce the original lyrics, in which the hero is a girl. 'The House of the Rising Sun' is thought to refer either to a brothel or a women's prison. The song has also been recorded by Joan Baez, Bob Dylan and Nina Simone.

Chord diagrams

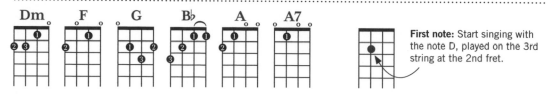

First note: Start singing with the note D, played on the 3rd string at the 2nd fret.

Strumming

'The House of the Rising Sun' is in 6/8 time. This means that you can think of each bar as having two beats, each divided into three counts: '**1**, 2, 3, **2**, 2, 3'. The counting shown against the first line would look as follows (with the bar starting on 'is'):

These lines are to show where one bar ends and the next begins.

Count:		1 – 2 – 3 2 – 2 – 3	1 – 2 – 3 2 – 2 – 3	1 – 2 – 3 2 – 2 – 3	1 – 2 – 3 2 – 2 – 3
Sing:	There	is_____ a	house_____ in	New Or - leans	

The strumming pattern you use needs to work with the 6/8 time. At its simplest, you could just strum down on the two beats of the bar that are the counts marked in red above. Alternatively, you could strum down on all the counts. This would mean that you would strum down six times in each bar (without doing any upward strums).

A third and more interesting option involves slightly more brisk strumming up and down, and requires that you count 'and' between each of the counts above. To get this strum right, you need to count the bar as '**1**, and, 2, and, 3, and, **2**, and, 2, and, 3, and'. Based on this counting, the strum looks as follows in rhythm notation (see page 90):

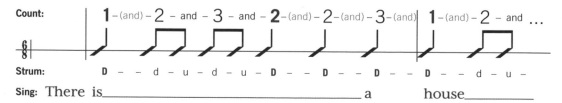

You strum up on only some of the 'and' counts and skip the other (greyed-out) ones. It is worth trying to master this strum as it works well with the 6/8 time signature.

     Dm F   G   **B**♭

1. There is a house in New Orleans

     Dm   F   A   A7

They call the Rising Sun.

     Dm   F   G   B♭

It's been the ruin of many a poor girl,

    Dm   A7   Dm

And me, O God, for one.

2. If (Dm) I had (F) listened what (G) Mamma said, (B♭)
I'd have (Dm) been at (F) home to-(A)day. (A7)
(Dm) Being so (F) young and (G) foolish, poor (B♭) boy,
Let a (Dm) rambler (A7) lead me a-(Dm)stray.

3. Go (Dm) tell my (F) baby (G) sister (B♭)
Never (Dm) do like (F) I have (A) done. (A7)
To (Dm) shun that (F) house in (G) New Orleans (B♭)
They (Dm) call the (A7) Rising (Dm) Sun.

4. My (Dm) mother, (F) she's a (G) tailor; (B♭)
She (Dm) sold those (F) new blue (A) jeans. (A7)
My (Dm) sweetheart, (F) he's a (G) drunkard, Lord, (B♭)
Drinks (Dm) down in (A7) New Or-(Dm)leans.

5. The (Dm) only (F) thing a (G) drunkard needs (B♭)
Is a (Dm) suitcase (F) and a (A) trunk. (A7)
The (Dm) only (F) time he's (G) satisfied (B♭)
Is (Dm) when he's (A7) on a (Dm) drunk.

6. Fills (Dm) his (F) glasses (G) to the brim, (B♭)
(Dm) Passes (F) them (A) around. (A7)
(Dm) Only (F) pleasure he gets (G) out of life (B♭)
Is (Dm) hoboin' from (A7) town to (Dm) town.

7. One (Dm) foot is (F) on the (G) platform (B♭)
And the (Dm) other one (F) on the (A) train. (A7)
I'm (Dm) going (F) back to (G) New Orleans (B♭)
To (Dm) wear that (A7) ball and (Dm) chain.

8. (Dm) Going (F) back to (G) New Orleans, (B♭)
My (Dm) race is (F) almost (A) run. (A7)
Going (Dm) back to (F) spend the (G) rest of my days (B♭)
Be-(Dm)neath that (A7) Rising (Dm) Sun.

Greensleeves

Traditional

This English ballad, a tale of unrequited love – a common theme in Renaissance and medieval love songs – suits the ukulele as it would have been played on an instrument with re-entrant tuning (see page 82).

Playing notes

You can play this as an instrumental using the music/tabs (see pages 92–3 and pages 95–6) or sing it as a song, strumming the chords (see Chord Finder on the inside covers). You could try a duet, with one playing the tune while the other strums the chord once at the start of each bar.

The instrumental sounds best if you play the notes at the start of each bar as a slow downward strum. You want to hear all the strings ring out in turn as you strum. The trickiest fingering is in the bars marked *. Strum as you hold the position shown in black on the right. Then remove your fourth finger to play the next note on the 1st string with your first finger forming a 'barre' (shown in grey). See page 102 for more on barre chords.

A - las my love__ ye do me wrong to cast me off__ dis - cour - teous - ly, And

I have lov - ed you so long__ de - light - ing in your com - pa - ny.

Green sleeves was all my joy._____ Green - sleeves was my de - light.

Green - sleeves was my heart of gold__ and who but my la - dy Green - sleeves.

The Skye Boat Song

Words by Sir Harold Boulton

Recounting the story of Bonnie Prince Charlie's escape to the Isle of Skye with Flora McDonald following the defeat of his largely Scottish army by the English in 1746, this song was written long after those events. It was published in 1884 by Harold Boulton and Anne MacLeod, though MacLeod reportedly based the melody on a sea shanty she had heard. The Sixties version by the Corries is worth checking out online.

Chord diagrams

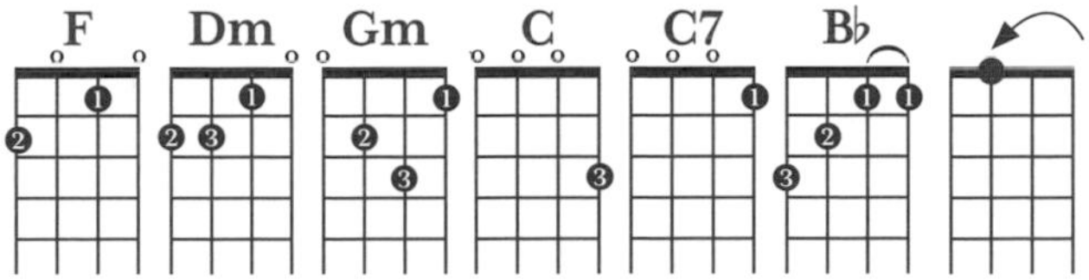

F   Dm   Gm   C   C7   B♭

Strumming

First note: Start singing with the note C, which is the open 3rd string.

Simple strumming works best here: a gentle downstroke on the first beat of each bar. Strumming on the red lyrics would therefore go like this: 'Speed, bonnie boat, like a bird on the wing, ...'

                   F   Dm   Gm   C
Chorus: *Speed, bonnie boat, like a bird on the wing,*

F   Gm   C7
Onward! the sailors cry;

F   Dm   Gm   C
Carry the lad that's born to be King

F   B♭   F
Over the sea to Skye.

1. **(Dm)** Loud the winds howl, **(Gm)** loud the waves roar,
(Dm) Thunderclaps rend the air;
(Dm) Baffled, our foes **(Gm)** stand by the shore,
(Dm) Follow they will not **(Gm)** dare. **(C7)**

Chorus

2. **(Dm)** Though the waves leap, **(Gm)** soft shall ye sleep,
(Dm) Ocean's a royal bed.
(Dm) Rocked in the deep, **(Gm)** Flora will keep
(Dm) Watch by your weary **(Gm)** head. **(C7)**

Chorus

3. **(Dm)** Burned are their homes, **(Gm)** exile and death
(Dm) Scatter the loyal men;
(Dm) Yet ere the sword **(Gm)** cool in the sheath
(Dm) Charlie will come **(Gm)** again. **(C7)**

Chorus

Molly Malone

Words and music by James Yorkston

Often known as 'Cockles and Mussels', this tune has been recorded by the Dubliners, U2 and Sinead O'Connor. It's worth learning the simple lyrics by heart and belting them out in a lusty singalong style. The story is pure myth: no one has successfully linked Molly with a real person, and the song's not a traditional Irish ballad but a Victorian music hall favourite by Scottish composer James Yorkston.

Chord diagrams

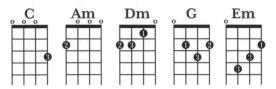

(Almost) First note: The low G for the first word, 'In', can't be played on a ukulele with re-entrant tuning (see page 82). But the next note (for the word 'Dublin's') is a C. This is the open 3rd string.

Strumming

This song is in 3/4 time, which means that each bar has three beats in it. So you need to strum a rhythm that fits with the count of '1, 2, 3, 1, 2, 3 ...' You could simply strum down on each beat of the bar, which would mean you strummed down once on each beat of 'Du - blin's fair ...'.

A more interesting alternative might be to try the strum shown below in the rhythm notation (see page 90). You could try putting the emphasis on the first beat of every bar, as indicated by the red.

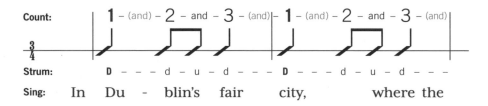

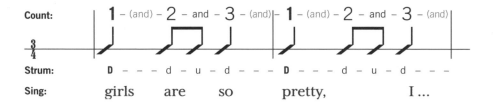

    C   Am
1. In Dublin's fair city,

         Dm   G
Where the girls are so pretty,

  C   Em   Dm   G
I first set my eyes on sweet Molly Malone,

       C   Am
As she wheeled her wheelbarrow

      Dm   G
Through streets broad and narrow,

      C   Em   Dm G   C
Crying, 'Cockles and mussels, alive, alive, oh!'

'A-(C)*live, alive,* (Am) *oh,*
'A-(Dm)*live, alive,* (G) *oh,'*
Crying, (C) *'Cockles and* (Em) *mussels, a-*(Dm)*live, a-*(G)*live,* (C) *oh!'*

2. She (C) was a fish-(Am)monger,
But (Dm) sure 'twas no (G) wonder,
For (C) so were her (Em) father and (Dm) mother be-(G)fore.
And they (C) each wheeled their (Am) barrow
Through (Dm) streets broad and (G) narrow,
Crying, (C) 'Cockles and (Em) mussels, a-(Dm)live, a-(G)live, (C) oh!'

'A-(C)*live, alive,* (Am) *oh,*
'A-(Dm)*live, alive,* (G) *oh,'*
Crying, (C) *'Cockles and* (Em) *mussels, a-*(Dm)*live, a-*(G)*live,* (C) *oh!'*

3. She (C) died of a (Am) fever,
And (Dm) no one could (G) save her,
And (C) that was the (Em) end of sweet (Dm) Molly Ma-(G)lone.
Now, her (C) ghost wheels her (Am) barrow
Through (Dm) streets broad and (G) narrow,
Crying, (C) 'Cockles and (Em) mussels, a-(Dm)live, a-(G)live, (C) oh!'

'A-(C)*live, alive,* (Am) *oh,*
'A-(Dm)*live, alive,* (G) *oh,'*
Crying, (C) *'Cockles and* (Em) *mussels, a-*(Dm)*live, a-*(G)*live,* (C) *oh!'*

The John B. Sails

Folk traditional

This folk song about a disastrous sailing trip emerged from Nassau in the Bahamas around the turn of the 20th century. It was collected by folklorists Carl Sandburg and Alan Lomax, and has been recorded by many artists. Johnny Cash recorded it in 1959, and in 1966 the Beach Boys' version, 'Sloop John B', sold half a million copies worldwide in two weeks.

Chord diagrams

C   G7   F

(Almost) First note: The low G for the first words, 'Oh, we', can't be played on a ukulele with re-entrant tuning (see page 82). But the next note (for the word 'come') is an E. This is the open 2nd string.

Strumming

For a Caribbean ditty like this, a good strumming pattern is the calypso strum, which is explained on page 99.

                  C
1. Oh, we come on the sloop John B.,

My gran'fadder an' me.
                              G7
Round Nassau Town we did roam,
               C   F
Drinking all night, we got in a fight,
C   G7   C
I feel so break-up, I want to go home!

                         C
Chorus: *So hoist up the John B. sails,*

See how de main-s'l set,
                                        G7
Send for de Capt'n ashore, lemme go home!
               C   F
Lemme go home! Lemme go home!
    C   G7   C
I feel so break-up, I want to go home!

2. De (C) first mate, he got drunk,
Break up de people's trunk.
Constable come aboard an' take him a-(G7)way.
Mr. Johnstone, (C) please let me a-(F)lone.
I (C) feel so break-up, (G7) I want to go (C) home!

Chorus

3. De (C) poor cook, he got fits,
Tro' 'way all de grits,
Den he took an' eat up all o' my (G7) corn!
Lemme go (C) home, I want to go (F) home!
Dis (C) is de worst trip (G7) since I been (C) born!

Chorus

Danny Boy

Words by Frederic Weatherly

This beautiful lament, written in 1910 and sung to the tune of the 'Londonderry Air', has been recorded by artists as diverse as Sam Cooke, Johnny Cash, Elvis Presley, Sinead O'Connor and the Pogues.

Main chords

Optional chords (in paler colour within lyrics)

G7   C   C7   F   Am   Dm   Fm   F6

(Almost) First note:
As a low B can't be played on a ukulele with re-entrant tuning (see page 82), the first note to sing is C for the second word 'Danny', which is played on the open 3rd string.

Strumming

The church lick, aka bluegrass strumming (see page 90), works pretty well for this.

```
G7          C                    C7        F
Oh, Danny boy, the pipes, the pipes are calling
G7          C         Am              Dm   G7
From glen to glen, and down the mountain side.
            C                C7    Dm F   Fm/G7
The summer's gone, and all the roses falling,
            C        G7          C     G7
It's you, it's you must go and I must bide.
            C        F              C
But come ye back when summer's in the meadow,
G7          C      F                    F6/G7   G7
Or when the valley's hushed and white with snow,
            C      F      Dm   C
It's I'll be here in sunshine or in shadow,—
F6/F        C          F6/F        C
Oh, Danny boy, Oh Danny boy, I love you so!
```

2. (G7) But when ye (C) come, and all the (C7) flowers are (F) dying,
(G7) If I am (C) dead, as (Am) dead I well may (Dm) be, (G7)
Ye'll come and (C) find the place where (C7) I am (Dm) ly-(F)ing, (Fm/G7)
And kneel and (C) say an (G7) Ave there for (C) me. (G7)
And I shall (C) hear, though (F) soft you tread (C) above me,
(G7) And all my (C) grave will (F) warmer, sweeter (F6/G7) be, (G7)
For you will (C) bend and (F) tell me (Dm) that you (C) love me,
(F6/F) And I shall (C) sleep in peace un-(F6/F)til you come to (C) me!

Waltzing Matilda

Words by Banjo Paterson

This Australian folk song tells the sad tale of a swagman, or itinerant worker, who kills himself rather than be arrested for theft. 'Waltzing' was slang for 'wandering', and a 'Matilda' was the swagman's bag. The lyrics were written in 1895 by poet Banjo Paterson to a Scottish tune played on the zither by Christina Macpherson while both were staying at Macpherson's family bush station in Queensland.

Chord diagrams

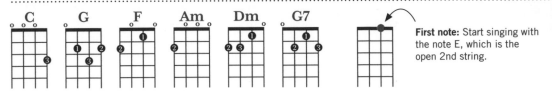

First note: Start singing with the note E, which is the open 2nd string.

Strumming

This song is in 4/4 time, which means that each bar has four beats in it.
A good strumming pattern is the church lick, aka bluegrass strumming (see page 90). Written in rhythm notation, it looks like this:

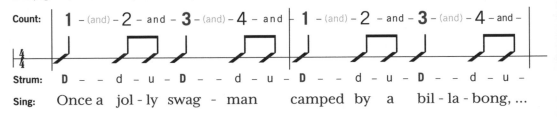

Count: 1 – (and) – 2 – and – 3 – (and) – 4 – and ⌐ 1 – (and) – 2 – and – 3 – (and) – 4 – and –

Strum: D – – d – u – D – – d – u – D – – d – u – D – – d – u –

Sing: Once a jol - ly swag - man   camped by a   bil - la - bong, ...

<pre>
        C   G   C   F
1. Once a jolly swagman camped by a billabong,

C   Am   Dm   G7
Under the shade of a coolibah tree.

            C   G   Am   F
And he sang as he watched and waited till his billy boiled,

C   Am   G7   C
'Who'll come a-waltzing Matilda, with me?'
</pre>

```
            C                    F
Chorus: Waltzing Matilda, waltzing Matilda,
C           Am         Dm        G7
You'll come a-waltzing Matilda, with me.
            C        E7          Am          F
And he sang as he watched and waited till his billy boiled,
C           Am         G7          C
'You'll come a-waltzing Matilda, with me.'
```

2. (C) Down came a (G) jumbuck to (C) drink at that (F) billabong;
(C) Up jumped the (Am) swagman and (Dm) grabbed him with (G7) glee.
And he (C) sang as he (G) shoved that (Am) jumbuck in his (F) tucker bag,
(C) 'You'll come a-(Am)waltzing Ma-(G7)tilda, with (C) me.'

(C) *Waltzing Matilda,* (F) *waltzing Matilda,*
(C) *You'll come a-*(Am)*waltzing Ma-*(Dm)*tilda, with* (G7) *me.*
And he (C) *sang as he* (E7) *shoved that* (Am) *jumbuck in his* (F) *tucker bag,*
(C) *'You'll come a-*(Am)*waltzing Ma-*(G7)*tilda, with* (C) *me.'*

3. (C) Up rode the (G) squatter, (C) mounted on his (F) thoroughbred;
(C) Down came the (Am) troopers, (Dm) one, two and (G7) three.
(C) 'Whose is that (G) jumbuck you've (Am) got in your (F) tucker bag?
(C) 'You'll come a-(Am)waltzing Ma-(G7)tilda, with (C) me.'

(C) *Waltzing Matilda,* (F) *waltzing Matilda,*
(C) *You'll come a-*(Am)*waltzing Ma-*(Dm)*tilda, with* (G7) *me.*
(C) *'Whose is that* (E7) *jumbuck you've* (Am) *got in your* (F) *tucker bag?*
(C) *'You'll come a-*(Am)*waltzing Ma-*(G7)*tilda, with* (C) *me.'*

4. (C) Up jumped the (G) swagman and (C) sprang into the (F) billabong;
(C) 'You'll never (Am) take me (Dm) alive!' said (G7) he.
And his (C) ghost may be (G) heard as you (Am) pass by that (F) billabong:
(C) 'Who'll come a-(Am)waltzing Ma-(G7)tilda, with (C) me?'

(C) *Waltzing Matilda,* (F) *waltzing Matilda,*
(C) *You'll come a-*(Am)*waltzing Ma-*(Dm)*tilda, with* (G7) *me.*
(C) *And his ghost may be* (E7) *heard as you* (Am) *pass by that* (F) *billabong:*
(C) *'Who'll come a-*(Am)*waltzing Ma-*(G7)*tilda, with* (C) *me?'*

Oh My Darling, Clementine

Folk traditional

This is a comical cowboy ballad that dates from the gold-rush days of the 19th century. Yes, the lyrics are completely ridiculous, but you'd have to be a real party pooper not to join in when this one gets going round the campfire.

Chord diagrams

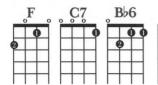

First note:
The first note to sing is an F, played on the 1st fret of the 2nd string.

Fingerpicking

Since the chords are so easy for this song, why not try picking the strings rather than strumming them? You should go back over pages 103–6 of the How to Play section to familiarize yourself with this. Since the time signature of this song is 3/4 time (three beats in a bar), you'll need to use the 3/4-time picking pattern shown on page 106.

     F
1. In a cavern, in a canyon,
        C7
Excavating for a mine,
             F
Dwelt a miner, forty-niner,
  B♭6   **C7**   **F**
And his daughter, Clementine.

                F
Chorus: *Oh my darling, oh my darling,*
            C7
Oh my darling, Clementine!
            F
Thou art lost and gone forever;
  B♭6   **C7** **F**
Dreadful sorry, Clementine.

2. Light she (**F**) was, and like a fairy,
And her shoes were number (**C7**) nine
Herring boxes, without (**F**) topses;
Sandals (**B♭6**) were for (**C7**) Clemen-(**F**)tine.

Chorus

3. Drove she (**F**) ducklings to the water
Ev'ry morning just at (**C7**) nine,
Hit her foot against a (**F**) splinter,
Fell in-(**B♭6**)to the (**C7**) foaming (**F**) brine.

Chorus

4. Ruby (**F**) lips above the water,
Blowing bubbles soft and (**C7**) fine;
But, alas, I was no (**F**) swimmer,
So I (**B♭6**) lost my (**C7**) Clemen-(**F**)tine.

Chorus

5. In a (**F**) churchyard near the canyon,
Where the myrtle boughs en-(**C7**)twine,
There grow roses in their (**F**) posies,
Ferti-(**B♭6**)lized by (**C7**) Clemen-(**F**)tine.

Chorus

6. In a (**F**) tavern in the canyon,
Drinking beer and lots of (**C7**) wine,
Sat a miner, forty-(**F**)niner,
Grieving (**B♭6**) over (**C7**) Clemen-(**F**)tine.

Chorus

7. How I (**F**) missed her, how I missed her,
How I missed my Clemen-(**C7**)tine,
Till I kissed her little (**F**) sister,
And for-(**B♭6**)got my (**C7**) Clemen-(**F**)tine.

Chorus

My Bonnie Lies Over the Ocean

Folk traditional

First published in 1881, the true origins of this Scottish folk song are unknown. A great rock'n'roll version, called 'My Bonnie', was recorded in 1961 by the Beatles with Tony Sheridan on vocals. You could try playing a version like this (look it up on YouTube), complete with the rock'n'roll change of tempo after the first verse, when it goes from 3/4 to 4/4 time and changes key from A to the key of C shown here.

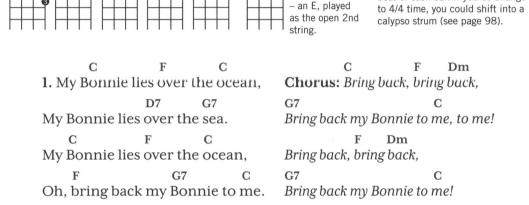

Chord diagrams

C   F   D7   G7   Dm

(Almost) First note: As the first note ('My') is too low for the uke, start with the second ('Bonnie') – an E, played as the open 2nd string.

Strumming

The original is in 3/4 time, which means you count '1, 2, 3, 1, 2, 3 ...'. Start with a simple strum on the first beat of each bar. If you do change to 4/4 time, you could shift into a calypso strum (see page 98).

```
        C          F        C
1. My Bonnie lies over the ocean,
            D7       G7
My Bonnie lies over the sea.
        C          F        C
My Bonnie lies over the ocean,
        F           G7       C
Oh, bring back my Bonnie to me.
```

```
                C        F      Dm
Chorus: Bring back, bring back,
G7                        C
Bring back my Bonnie to me, to me!
                   F      Dm
Bring back, bring back,
G7                        C
Bring back my Bonnie to me!
```

2. Last (C) night as I (F) lay on my (C) pillow,
Last night as I (D7) lay on my (G7) bed,
Last (C) night as I (F) lay on my (C) pillow,
I (F) dreamt that my (G7) Bonnie was (C) dead.

Chorus

3. Oh, (C) blow the winds (F) o'er the (C) ocean,
And blow the winds (D7) o'er the (G7) sea.
Oh, (C) blow the winds (F) o'er the (C) ocean,
And (F) bring back my (G7) Bonnie to (C) me.

Chorus

4. The (C) winds have blown (F) over the (C) ocean,
The winds have blown (D7) over the (G7) sea.
The (C) winds have blown (F) over the (C) ocean,
And (F) brought back my (G7) Bonnie to (C) me.

Chorus

Resources

Internet Resources

Here is a small selection of the many uke-based websites.

UKULELE UNDERGROUND
www.ukuleleunderground.com
Founded in 2007 by three hip young Hawaiians, this is probably the slickest uke site on the web. The boys combine enthusiasm with professionalism, and the site is vibrant, well designed and well maintained. You can sign up for courses, watch their videos, buy carefully selected uke products, and join the busy forum. They also have a great Ukulele Underground channel on YouTube.

FLEA MARKET MUSIC
www.fleamarketmusic.com
Jim Beloff's site offers an online store selling Fluke ukuleles, plus Jim's fantastic books and CDs. There is also a community area, a tuner, a resources section and a comprehensive links page. The site's Marketplace is a good place to look if you are considering buying a vintage ukulele.

UKULELE HUNT
www.ukulelehunt.com
A terrific resource for uke players, Alistair Wood's Ukulele Hunt offers lessons, chords, e-books and loads of song sheets.

UKEFARM
www.ukefarm.com
A serious-minded site that offers a radio show where you can hear John King playing Bach and other delights. There are also chord sheets and videos here.

SHEEP-ENTERTAINMENT
www.ukulele.nl
An eccentric Dutch ukulele site that features lots of play-along songs, a ukulele chord finder, plus a tuner.

THE MACCAFERRI ISLANDER CHORDMASTER
www.chordmaster.org
The chordmaster was a push-button device that could be attached to your ukulele. This fansite was created by Antoine Carolus, and also showcases his collection of plastic ukuleles from the Fifties.

IAN WHITCOMB
www.picklehead.com/ian.html
News on Tin Pan Alley expert and uke player Ian Whitcomb's latest books, gigs and other uke-related projects.

UKULELE STRUMMERS
www.ukulelestrummers.com
A laid-back Hawaiian site that includes some excellent tutorials.

UKULELE THAI
www.ukulelethai.com
The Thais have uploaded some fantastic uke videos on this site.

THE GEORGE FORMBY SOCIETY
www.georgeformby.co.uk
All the latest news on George Formby conventions and events, plus historical and musical resources on the grinning Lancastrian sensation.

UKULELE MIKE
www.ukulelemikelynch.com
Ukulele Mike is a cheerful teacher who spreads the word of the uke though YouTube tutorials, his own website, public performances, DVDs, e-books and a radio station, KUKE.

DOMINATOR
www.dominator.ukeland.com
Dominator is a ukulele teacher who regularly posts tabs on his site. He has also recorded a number of YouTube videos.

MOUNTAIN APPLE
www.mountainapplecompany.com
Site of the famous Hawaiian record company, home of IZ® and many more.

Further Reading and Viewing

Explore the ukulele more deeply with this list of reading matter and films.

THE 'UKULELE: A HISTORY
Jim Tranquada and John King
University of Hawai'i Press, 2012
This is *the* outstanding scholarly work on the history of the ukulele. The result of seven years' research and study, it is painstakingly notated and sourced. The book's co-author John King (see page 68) sadly died before it was published. Jim Tranquada is a great-great-grandson of ukulele pioneer Augusto Dias.

THE UKULELE: A VISUAL HISTORY
Jim Beloff
Backbeat Books, 2003
Beloff's uke book is a lively trawl through the fantastic iconography of the ukulele over the ages. It contains fascinating research and is stuffed with wonderful images.

UKULELE FOR DUMMIES
Alistair Wood
John Wiley & Sons, 2011
One of the best teach-yourself manuals we've come across. Extremely thorough, in our opinion it's a must-have. Its author runs ukulelehunt.com.

HAWAIIAN MUSIC AND MUSICIANS
ed. George S. Kanahele and John Berger
Mutual Publishing, 2012
The ultimate encyclopedia for anyone interested in Hawaiian music. This is a new expanded edition of the original 1979 publication.

THE UKULELE: THE WORLD'S FRIENDLIEST INSTRUMENT
Daniel Dixon
Gibbs Smith Inc., 2011
A jaunty history, featuring interviews with uke gurus Ian Whitcomb, Jim Beloff and Mike DaSilva, this book was written by a uke player who sadly died before publication. With some great pictures, it's another must-have for your ukulele library.

THE UKULELE ENTERTAINER: POWERFUL POINTERS FOR PLAYERS AND PERFORMERS
Ralph Shaw
Prol Thacker, 2012
A book of tips and tricks for anyone who performs in public with their uke, or would like to. The virtuoso player James Hill has called Shaw 'a true entertainer and a gifted teacher'.

FACING FUTURE
Dan Kois
Continuum Books, 2010
Thorough song-by-song analysis of Israel Kamakawiwo'ole's great album *Facing Future*, with lots of biographical information.

KAMUKE: UKULELE MAGAZINE
ed. Cameron Murray
www.kamuke.com
Based in Sydney, Australia, this mag is well worth subscribing to as it will keep you up to date with the latest news in the ukulele world. Every issue features uke players, manufacturers, pro tips and reviews of relevant books, films and records.

FRANK SKINNER ON GEORGE FORMBY (2011)
A warm, witty and informative documentary about Formby's life and legacy. Skinner is an engaging host, and in the film he plays the ukulele on stage at a quarterly convention of the George Formby Society in Blackpool. First broadcast by the BBC, it can be viewed on YouTube.

MIGHTY UKE: THE AMAZING COMEBACK OF A MUSICAL UNDERDOG
www.mightyukemovie.com
An exploration of today's global ukulele culture and its unifying power, this documentary has won a clutch of awards at film festivals. 'The most charming documentary I have ever seen,' said CBC Radio of this Canadian-produced film.

Acknowledgements

We are deeply indebted to all the various ukulele people around the world who have generously given up their time to correct our errors, give quotes and send us pictures. In particular, we would like to thank the following: Mark Reddy for sharing his expertise and allowing us to photograph the rare vintage ukes from his Ravenscrag Collection; Antoine Carolus (UkeHeidi – chordmaster.org) for the photos of his collection of plastic ukuleles from the Fifties and Sixties, and for correcting several errors; Cameron Murray, editor of *Kamuke* magazine, for his interview and various hints and tips along the way; Danny Wootton for letting us refer to his Idler Academy Uke Course and for checking over the How to Play section; John Marsden for sending us pictures of Hawaiian groups from the Forties and for further reading tips; George Hinchliffe of the Ukulele Orchestra of Great Britain for the interview; Jim Beloff for sending us pictures and checking the text; Paul Moore of Ukuleles for Peace for checking the text and coming all the way to Tom's village; Chris Goodwin of the Lute Society for providing materials on re-entrant tuning; James Hill for checking our facts; Sherrie Hoyer for the May Singhi Breen photo (check out Sherrie's online store at www.mandolinbabe.biz); Ian Whitcomb for use of his portrait (check out Ian's book *Ukulele Heroes*); Catherine St Germans for Hawaii-based picture research; our editor, Natalie Hunt, and Richard Atkinson and Xa Shaw Stewart at Bloomsbury; our copy editors, Christopher Hussey and Trish Burgess; our agents, Cat Ledger (Tom) and Patrick Walsh (Gavin); and, finally, Victoria Hull and Liz Pickering. We have also relied heavily on the superior knowledge of others when preparing this book. Three volumes in particular have been invaluable: *The 'Ukulele: A History* by Jim Tranquada and John King; *Hawaiian Music and Musicians: An Illustrated History* edited by George S. Kanahele; and *The Ukulele: An Illustrated History* by Jim Beloff.

Picture Credits

Title page: © Honolulu Museum of Art. *Background images 16, 18–19, 22, 26, 31, 32, 41–4, 58, 63–6, 68, 71, 73, 74:* © Markovka/Shutterstock.com. *10 (middle):* From the collection of Graham Ovenden. *10–11 (bottom):* Library of Congress, LC-DIG-pga-02377. *12 (top):* From *A History of Madeira* by William Combe (R. Ackermann, London, 1821). *12 (bottom):* Drawn by Alfred T. Agate; engraved by J.A. Rolph. *13 (top):* Instrument courtesy of The Ravenscrag Collection. *13 (bottom):* Library of Congress, LC-USZ62-61318. *14 (all images):* Hawaii State Archives. *15 (top):* Instrument courtesy of The Ravenscrag Collection. *15 (bottom):* Hawaii State Library. *17 (top):* Hawaii State Archives. *17 (bottom):* Library of Congress, HABS HI,2-HONLU,8--44. *18 (portrait), 19:* Hawaii State Archives. *20:* Library of Congress, LC-DIG-ppmsca-28877. *21, 22 (portraits):* Hawaii State Archives. *23 (top):* © senlektomyum/Shutterstock.com. *23 (middle):* Hawaii State Archives. *23 (bottom):* Instrument courtesy of The Ravenscrag Collection. *24 (bottom):* Hawaii State Archives. *25 (both images):* Library of Congress, *(top)* LC-DIG-hec-18809. *26 (portrait):* Hawaiian Mission Houses Archives. *26 (cutting):* Hawaii State Library. *27 (bottom):* © Hulton Archive/Getty Images. *29 (bottom):* Instruments courtesy of The Ravenscrag Collection. *31 (portrait):* From the photo collection of Sherrie Hoyer. *33 (bottom):* Instrument courtesy of The Ravenscrag Collection. *34 (top):* © Hulton Archive/Getty Images. *34 (bottom):* Library of Congress, LC-USZ62-9614. *35 (all images):* © Elderly Instruments, photo by Dave Matchette. *36:* © Hal Roach/MGM/The Kobal Collection. *37:* © John Springer Collection/Corbis. *38:* Herbert Jenkins Limited, London, 1936. *39:* Instrument courtesy of The Ravenscrag Collection. *41 (portrait):* © Silver Screen Collection/Moviepix/Getty Images. *42:* © Fox Photos/Hulton Archive/Getty Images. *43:* © London Express/Hulton Archive/Getty Images. *44:* © Moviepix/Getty Images. *45:* Library of Congress, LC-USZ62-127112. *46:* All images courtesy John Marsden. *47 (television):* © R. Gino Santa Maria/Shutterstock.com. *47 (middle and bottom), 48–9 (all ukes), 50 (all images):* © Antoine Carolus/UkeHeidi. *52 (portrait):* © Hawaii Sons, Inc. *53:* © Tad Tamura. *54 (top):* © Antoine Carolus/UkeHeidi. *54 (bottom):* © Elderly Instruments, photo by Dave Matchette. *55:* United Artists/The Kobal Collection. *56 (uke):* © Antoine Carolus/UkeHeidi. *56 (bottom):* © Bernard Gotfryd/Premium Archive/Getty Images. *57 (top):* Courtesy of Ian Whitcomb. *57 (bottom):* © Elderly Instruments, photo by Dave Matchette. *58:* © NBC Universal/Getty Images. *60 (top):* © Colleen Ricci. *61 (top):* © Sarah Worker. *61 (bottom):* © Nigel Barklie. *62, 63, 64:* Courtesy of The Mountain Apple Company, mountainapplecompany.com. *67 (top):* © Aaron Kotowski. *67 (laptop):* ixpert/Shutterstock.com. *68 (background):* © Markovka/Shutterstock.com. *68:* © B.J. Morgan/Museum of Making Music, Carlsbad, Calif. *69 (bottom):* © Sweet Hollywaiians. *70 (all photos):* © Chuck Moore, Moore Bettah Ukuleles, moorebettahukes.com. *71:* © Merri Cyr. *72 (all images):* © Paul Moore/Ukuleles for Peace. *73:* © Andy Catlin on behalf of the Queen's Hall, Edinburgh. *74:* © Kevin Kelly. *75 (top):* © Matthew Hensby. *75 (bottom):* © Michael DaSilva, DaSilva Ukulele Company, ukemaker.com. *78–115 (all photographs and illustrations):* © Gavin Pretor-Pinney.

Index

Page numbers in *italic* refer to the illustrations